D0506800

MAURICE FABRE   VOL. 7 | a history of land transportation

This book was designed and produced by Erik Nitsche International, S.A., Geneva. It was printed and bound in Switzerland by Heliogravure Centrale, Lausanne. The engravings were made by Heliogravure Centrale, Lausanne. The text paper is white gravure 140 gr/m². This book is published simultaneously in Canada by McClelland & Stewart Ltd., 25 Hollinger Road, Toronto 16. The Library of Congress has catalogued this volume of The New Illustrated Library of Science and Invention under card number 63-10476. Suggested Decimal Classification for this series is 500.

First edition - August, 1963
H-4543

Translation by Arnold Rosin

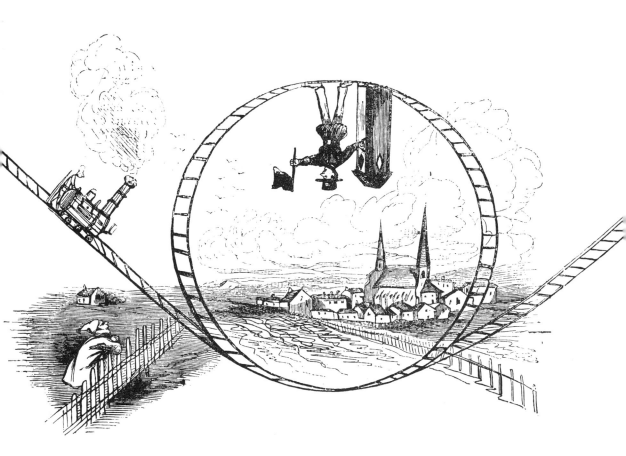

a history of land transportation

*Designed and produced
by Erik Nitsche*

THE NEW ILLUSTRATED LIBRARY OF SCIENCE AND INVENTION

*Hawthorn Books Inc.
Publishers, New York*

contents

On September 1, 1962, Glenn Leasher of Wichita, Kansas, was watching the morning sun glistening on the white desert sands of Bonneville Flats. Next to him stood a lightning-fast monster with a pointed nose and a low, streamlined body. It was the "Infinity," equipped with a Sabre F-86 aircraft engine of 8,000 horsepower. Leasher was determined to push it beyond the world speed record of 396 miles per hour established by Sir John Cobb on September 1, 1947. The "Infinity," and Leasher himself, were about to make automotive history.

As Leasher fastened his helmet before entering his powerful racer he looked like a warrior. In a sense he was a warrior, one of many who in the long history of the automobile have fought to beat a record, to win acceptance for some new idea, to perfect a machine, or simply to make the cussed thing go. For the history of the automobile is above all a history of obstacles overcome, of improvements made, of dreams turned into inventions—and of countless failures too. In this history there is nothing climactic, like the first explosion of the atomic bomb. Instead there is a long succession of small events, each important in itself—the mating of steam (and later of the gasoline engine) to a wheeled vehicle, the invention of the pneumatic tire, the "macad-amizing" of the roads in the early nineteenth century, the success of the four-cycle engine, Henry Ford's production line, even the latest attempt to beat the latest record.

And it is the same with land transportation in general. Who can say who invented the wheel, the chariot, the stagecoach, the tram, the electric locomotive? Who, for that matter, can say who invented the automobile? Was it Cugnot with his lumbering "fardier" of 1769? Was it Trevithick with his steam carriage of 1801, or the Bollées with their steam car of 1813? Or Benz and Daimler with their first successful internal combustion gasoline engine cars of 1886? It depends what you mean by an automobile.

In any case it has been a long and fascinating history, with one form of transportation competing against another. It started with man's two feet—a most efficient, if slow, form of transportation—soon supplemented by the sledge or travois. With civilization the horse-drawn cart, chariot, hooded wagon, and carriage emerged; and with these basic forms of land transportation man was content for thousands of years. Then in a burst of creativity he invented the steam car, the steam train, the bicycle, the tram, the electric locomotive, and finally that miracle, the automobile. For a long time the railroad was king; for a short time, the bicycle dominated the open road. But in the end the gasoline automobile won out over everything. It has killed off the horse and carriage, the steam and electric automobile have succumbed, the bicycle has almost been pushed off the roads and the tram out of the cities. With the aid of its big brothers, the truck and autobus, the automobile has even robbed the railroad of much of its traffic and most of its glory. There are now some 100 million automobiles in the world. Soon there may be 500 million.

And so we come back inevitably to the automobile as the dominant form of land transportation today. Its numbers, of course, are staggering: over 200 million have been built in the United States alone since 1896. But its importance is far deeper. In the United States, where the automobile has achieved its greatest triumphs, the automotive industry is the nation's largest, and the entire economy is dependent upon it. Historically, the automobile has put the nation on wheels, making it mobile, and has thus helped to unify this great land mass into a single, homogeneous culture. It moved the farmer into the city, then dictated the form of the great modern metropolis itself, with its congested center and sprawling suburbs. And today it is helping to build the "super cities" of tomorrow, those extended belts of thickly-settled areas, one city merging into another, that are growing up along both coasts. The same thing is happening in Europe, where the automobile industry is booming, where some 15 million cars are in use and the number is increasing daily, where city is beginning to merge into city along the main routes. And after Europe, the rest of the world will soon be inundated.

There is not much glamor about the history of the automobile and of land transportation. Science fiction, enamored of space travel, ignores it. Yet land transportation is very much a part of our lives. Its history, indeed, is a stirring record of obstacles overcome, of improvements made, of dreams fulfilled.

Glenn Leasher's dream, however, never came true. Travelling at more than 372 miles per hour, the "Infinity" exploded into a thousand fragments. Leasher died; but others will try for Sir John Cobb's record.

2   Primitive painting showing chariot, with
spoked wheels, pulled by three horses. This ochre
painting, discovered in the Sahara in 1934 by
the Gautier-Reygasse mission, was apparently done
by the Garamantes 500-600 years before Christ.

What is ~~land~~ transportation? In the simplest definition it is going from one place to another, on foot, on horseback, in a ~~vehicle~~, at any speed, perhaps carrying something, perhaps not; but in any case moving from one place to another across the ~~land surfaces of the globe.~~

A simple definition indeed; but yet what a wealth of history, what startling contrasts can be found within the limits of this definition! ~~Land~~ transportation can mean the trip between one primitive village and the next for trade or war, or it can mean a journey from Paris to Moscow. It can mean a man on foot on a jungle trail carrying a maximum of 110 pounds on his back, or a modern locomotive hauling 220,000 pounds at 120 miles per hour. It can mean the immemorial caravan of laden asses making its slow way across deserts and over mountain passes, or the thunder of a passing freight train, a mile or two in length, carrying tons upon tons of varied goods from city to city.

While land transportation is an integral part of history, history itself, in point of fact, has often been determined by movement across the land—movement of conquering armies, of whole peoples in migration, of trade, or deputations. In the earliest stages of man's history the rate of progress in land transportation was incredibly slow. ~~Yet~~ from the beginning man was characterized by his urge to move from one place to another—in search of food (the hunting of animals), in order to attack his neighbors, or to find a wife in some friendly or not so friendly group. Hunting, pillage, abduction: these were man's primitive goals, since trade did not assume importance until much later. Force and violence, again, were often behind

the endless human migrations of early times, the stronger conquering the weaker, compelling the latter to move on and attack another group in a chain reaction which often altered the course of history.

From one point of view man was—and is—the most ridiculous of all animals, for on his own two feet he could travel scarcely more than three miles per hour, and he could carry only a relatively light load. Despite the flexibility of his physical structure, he was, compared to other animals, a limited creature. The gazelle was swifter, the tiger more agile, the bear stronger. But the human animal had certain hidden advantages which, slowly but surely, would bring him to the top of the heap. He had a big brain, capable of enormous development. He had a flexible hand structure, almost a tool in itself, with a thumb opposed to the fingers. He had learned to walk upright, freeing his hands for the use of tools. But above all he remained unspecialized, without the long trunk of the elephant, the neck of the giraffe, the horn of the rhinoceros, so that he could develop in any direction.

And develop he did. Under the guidance of his brain he began to evolve substitutes for his own severe limitations. At first he had dragged, rolled and hauled the things he needed, exactly like certain insects. He quickly realized, however, that if hauling had to be done, it might as well be done by others under his direction. Thus beasts of burden—wild asses, donkeys, goats, elephants, camels, reindeer, oxen, dogs, and buffaloes—first appeared in the history of land transportation. There were slaves too, since predatory man was not averse

to domesticating his enemies; but slaves proved to be far more useful as servants and workers than as beasts of burden.

Whether pulled by man or beast, the earliest land vehicle seems to have been the sledge. The remains of one of the oldest known, perhaps 7,000 years old, was found in a peat bog. Very possibly the sledge had its origin in a simple branch drawn behind a man or beast. Certain primitive peoples still use a Y-shaped, forked branch pulled by oxen. The Indian travois, a fixed, V-shaped framework of two poles fastened to a horse was much the same kind of device.

The sled we know today brings to mind the sound of sharpened runners gliding over ice or crunching through crisp snow, and the delicious speed of the descent when we were children. Four thousand years ago the Egyptians used much the same kind of vehicle, but with far heavier, blunter runners, to transport immense blocks of stone, some weighing as much as 800 or 900 tons, destined to be made into statues, obelisks, pyramids or sarcophagi.

The sledge was indeed a useful device, but it was of limited potentiality. The wheel, however, spelled progress. The oldest examples of the wheel date from the fourth millennium B.C. and are found in Mesopotamia among the Sumerians, Akkadians, Elamites, and Chaldeans (or Babylonians). Actually the Sumerians, an enterprising people who were the first in the world to reach the level of civilization, seem to have been the earliest to utilize the full wheel. At first this was merely three planks of wood, pegged together in a rough circle. Soon it was strengthened with a metal band, or tire, and finally hollowed out for lightness

3   Rameses III, mounted on a light chariot, hunts gazelles (12th century B.C.). This fast, horse-drawn version of the chariot came to Egypt during the Hyksos invasion (17th century B.C.).

and equipped with spokes. For a long time the wheeled chariot was reserved for the nobility and priesthood; its use for trade, or by the common people as carts or wagons, came much later.

The Sumerian chariot was a clumsy vehicle, probably drawn by small onagers, or wild asses. For well over a thousand years it changed very little, until the introduction of the horse from central Asia. Around the seventeenth century B.C. the light, swift, horse-drawn chariot made its appearance. Introduced into Egypt by the conquering Hyksos, it became the principal weapon of the warlike Assyrians, who eventually subdued most of the civilized world. Thereafter the war chariot—the chariot of Homer's heroes, of the armies of Egypt's New Kingdom, of the Persian hordes as well as of the classical Greeks, dominated the ancient world.

Again there was little change until the Romans, an eminently practical people with an enormous empire to administer, constructed a huge road system that for the first time made it possible to develop and use many other types of vehicles besides the war chariot. The Romans had some 20 different varieties of vehicle, from the two-wheeled *carpentum*, very light and fast (it had a leather hood to protect the driver), to the great four-wheeled *carruca* which would carry an entire family. Yet curiously enough the Romans still used a complicated, clumsy system of harnessing that had been conceived 3,000 years earlier for oxen. Nor did they develop forward wheels pivoted on a central axis for ease in turning, a device which is believed to have been invented by the barbarian Celts.

The earliest roads were in fact merely paths, often created to begin with by animals who used them to reach their watering places. Men thereafter took over, using the paths for hunting or widening them for travel. Thus in America the easiest trails across the Appalachian mountains were first picked out by the migrating hordes of buffaloes, who were in turn followed by the Indians and eventually by the westward-travelling pioneers. Parts of these primitive trails are still in use today. And the same thing happened in prehistoric Europe and Asia. Mingling with the animals in terrifying proximity, as portrayed so vividly in the cave paintings, early man followed their paths along the river banks and through the winding valleys, and as civilization advanced enlarged and consolidated these primitive trails into more substantial roads.

One of the most extraordinary routes of ancient times, perhaps the oldest in the world, was undoubtedly more trail than road throughout its great length; but the importance of the amber route was not thereby diminished, for during the Bronze Age it assured the transport of this warmly beautiful material (believed to have magical powers, but actually only a hardened resin), across all of Europe from the Italian Alps to Denmark. This oldest of trade routes passed through what is now Austria and along the Elbe, funnelling the ideas and artifacts of civilization to the barbarian north in exchange for the coveted amber.

Another trade artery of incredible length was the silk route from China. Only the Chinese manufactured this marvellous fabric, and in order to sell it to the Persians they extended

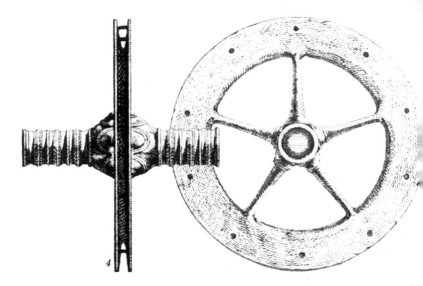

4

their routes across central Asia for more than 3,000 miles. In a later period, shortly before the birth of Christ, the Chou emperors built up an even larger and more complex road system, varying in size from the *ching*, a simple path, to the *lu*, on which three vehicles could pass at the same time.

The first real roads, those that were deliberately constructed and paved, were very short. Babylon under Nebuchadnezzar had its famous Procession Street, paved with large stones over a foundation of brick and asphalt, which led through the city to a substantial bridge across the Euphrates. To facilitate the transport of heavy blocks of stone the Egyptians built paved roads, short but very broad. Minoan Crete had its great causeway leading south from the palace of Cnossus to the Mediterranean shore while on the Greek mainland the Mycenaean roads, little more than pack trails, were reinforced with stone retaining walls and carried across streams on bridges with corbelled arches.

The first extensive road system, deliberately designed to facilitate imperial communications, was that of Darius the Great of Persia in the sixth century B.C. It was dominated by the Royal Road, with its stations for official messengers, which ran 1,500 miles from the Persian Gulf through Asia Minor and opened the way westward for the ill-fated attack upon Greece. This road system foreshadowed that of the greatest of Empires, the Roman. Learning the art of road construction, it seems, from the Etruscans and Carthaginians, the Romans eventually wove an incomparable network of roads that extended from Scotland to the

Sahara and from the Atlantic to the Persian Gulf, covering in all 52,700 miles. The Roman road was primarily a military road, built for the legions; but of course it was also used by couriers, officials, merchants and private travellers.

The average Roman road was from 18 to 24 feet wide, and was built with a high convex crown to shed water. It was firmly constructed with deep, well-drained foundations, sometimes as much as eight feet thick. At the bottom there might be a heavy foundation of stone slabs laid in mortar, leveled with sand, and above that successive layers of broken stone mixed with mortar, sand, and concrete, and finally a closely-laid top surfacing of heavy paving stones. Often side paths, separated from the main road by curbs, ran along its sides. And, as everybody knows, the Roman road ran straight, or at least as directly toward its objective as the configuration of the landscape would allow. If a village stood in its way, it might be razed. It would cut straight through forests, or would mount steeply up hills—for its gradient was often much more extreme than is common today.

Moreover, the Roman road was highly organized. About every 12 miles there was a relay station, about every 25 an inn, while ornate milestones and monuments marked its progress. Italy itself was served, in the southeast, by the Via Appia, broadest of Roman roads, in the northeast by the Via Flaminia, and in the northwest by the Via Aurelia, which led from Rome along the west coast of the Mediterranean as far as Antibes. The 25 or 30 roads which in one way or another

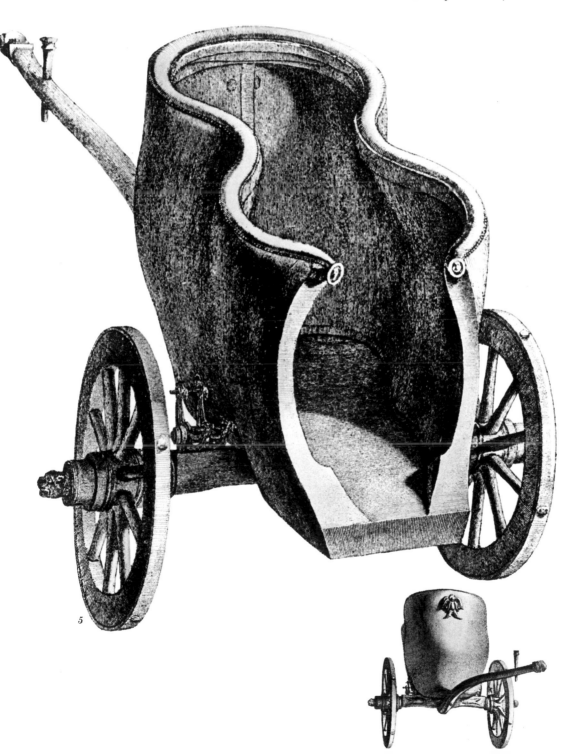

4   Ancient bronze wheel, seen in profile and front face, found near Toulouse. The very oldest pictures of wheels are found in Sumerian bas reliefs, dating from the fourth millennium B.C., which show a solid wheel made up of three segments of wood. Two thousand years later the spoked wheel appeared, as shown in Egyptian bas reliefs.

5   Etruscan bronze chariot, from an 18th century engraving by Piranesi. Note the light wheels. Chariots of this type were more manageable on the poor roads of the time.

5

6

7

linked the capital with the provinces included the Via Egnitia, which extended as far as Byzantium, and the Via Domitia, which followed Hannibal's route through Spain. Along these roads rolled vehicles like the *clabularia*, with its eight or ten oxen hauling as much as 220 pounds, and the *angaria* and *parangaria*, other types of heavy vehicles. Among lighter vehicles, there were the *reda*, *curruca*, and the *birota*.

The Roman roads appeared to be built for the ages; and it is certainly true that the world had to wait until the nineteenth century to improve upon them. They did, however, lack the resiliency and smoothness of asphalt and concrete, and in the end they proved to be as fragile as the Empire. Even before the fall of Rome, changes in temperature would loosen the stones, letting water into the foundations. Gradually falling apart, they would be repaired with a new, heavy coating of gravel and stone; but this meant frequent changes in thickness, which in turn made them increasingly subject to erosion. Compared to the light, easily repaired roads of our day, the very heaviness of their construction told against the Roman roads.

And then in 410 A.D. Rome itself was taken by the Goths and all that the Empire had contributed disappeared in its fall. A mounting wave of barbarians battered at the frontiers. Money could buy anything, including the dignity of the Emperor. But there was little left to buy, for gradually the cities had become isolated, and the roads which connected them with each other and with Rome fell into disuse. Many of them became quarries for the people who lived along their routes. Only a few survived into recent times.

There were other road systems worth remembering, and which suffered the same fate as that of Rome. By the time the Spanish conquistadores reached the west coast of South America, the Inca overlords had constructed a remarkable road network, covering 7,500 miles, which was used by the plumed "charquicuna" runners carrying the knotted ropes, or "quipus," containing the royal messages. Like the roads of Rome, only short sections of the Inca roads can still be traced.

It is difficult to construct roads on the desert; but with the camel man traced enduring roads which were as real as they were invisible. North Africa, from early times through the Middle Ages, saw some of the greatest of these routes. From Timbuctoo and Kano as far as Constantine, Carthage and Benghazi the caravans, often including as many as ten to 15,000 persons, plodded towards the Mediterranean, carrying gold, ivory, copper, resin, and musk, and returning with fabrics, pearls, spices and sugar. Originally the desert Tauregs had guarded the wells, served as guides, and had taken the tolls. Later the Arab merchants seized their great monopoly. Then the Portuguese, substituting the ship for the camel, changed the age-old pattern. Timbuctoo, which had once numbered almost 100,000 inhabitants, and other cities of the desert trade, were slowly strangled. The great trade routes were lost in the whirling sands, just as the bramble had gradually encroached upon the proud roads of ancient Rome.

6   *Horse wearing ornate Roman harness (drawing from a 19th century work).*
7   *Mounted archer, Roman light horse. Supreme footsoldiers, the Romans used auxiliary cavalry to repel barbarians.*

8 *Mechanical chariot from the triumphal parade given by the Emperor Maximilian I, in the early 16th century. This and other elaborate chariots, decorated with allegorical scenes, were moved forward by the efforts of men hidden inside, turning cranks.*

Like Janus, the Roman god of roads and beginnings, with his two faces, land transportation after the fall of Rome exhibited two successive, and quite opposite, faces. Both were concerned with what might be called mass migrations. The first was that of the great barbarian invasions and their aftermath, which caused an uprooting as savage as it was disorganized. This of course brought on a marked deterioration in the famous Roman road system. In 567 when the beautiful Galswinthe married Chilperic, she made the journey in a *bastern*, a crude, heavy-wheeled vehicle drawn by oxen, all that remained of the many different vehicles used in the Roman period. With the breakdown of Roman order not only the vehicles disappeared but many of the roads themselves.

The second face of Janus was that of the pilgrimage, a later and more hopeful migration which stimulated the recovery of civilization. Spurred on by religious faith, hundreds of thousands of pilgrims, before and during the crusades, moved in organized groups down through Europe and towards the east, some heading towards Santiago de Compostela or Rome—both difficult journeys across the Alps or the Pyrenees—and others aspiring to reach the Holy Land itself. At the same time the Arabs flocked towards Mecca. This continuous stream of pilgrims was joined by students, merchants, and mountebanks, and was often threatened by predatory barons and brigands. Most were on foot, many were lost; but the plodding pilgrim restored the idea of travel, of interchange; in a word, of land transportation.

10-13   *Earliest of all land vehicles, the sledge was used in many parts of the world. The example at the top was for the lazy traveller. Elegant Russian ladies took the air in Moscow in the one below it, while the more venturesome Lapps trusted themselves to reindeer. At bottom is a Danzig sledge.*

And following upon the pilgrims' travel and the crusades came a renewed interest in the Orient. Paris, Lisbon and Barcelona, London, Rome and Cologne, Vienna, Lübeck and Novgorod developed a taste for ginger, cinnamon, sugar, spikenard, ambergris, sandalwood, henna and ivory. By sea and by land caravans and convoys transported silk, spices, precious stones, tapestries, enamels and bronzes from east to west. The silk route was reopened by way of Hamadan, Samarkand and the Valley of the Fergana. Marco Polo, travelling to faroff Cathay in the thirteenth century, could not conceal his admiration for the Mongol emperor's network of mail and messenger routes, which covered his dominions from one frontier to the other.

In the thirteenth century, too, the first organized courier service appeared in Europe. About 1200 the University of Paris, a teeming beehive of students from many countries, established a mail and messenger service to carry the money and personal effects of its students to and from the city. Almost a century later this useful service was put under the royal protection by Philip the Fair, thus providing it with an official status. By 1502 the Thurn and Taxis family of Germany had managed to make the management of courier services their specialty, a specialty which remained in their hands until 1871. In 1516 courier lines were opened between Vienna and Brussels, and between Italy and the Netherlands.

Most travelling, whether by courier or by private individual, was done on horseback—or at the best in a clumsy descendant of Galswinthe's *bastern*—until the adoption, during

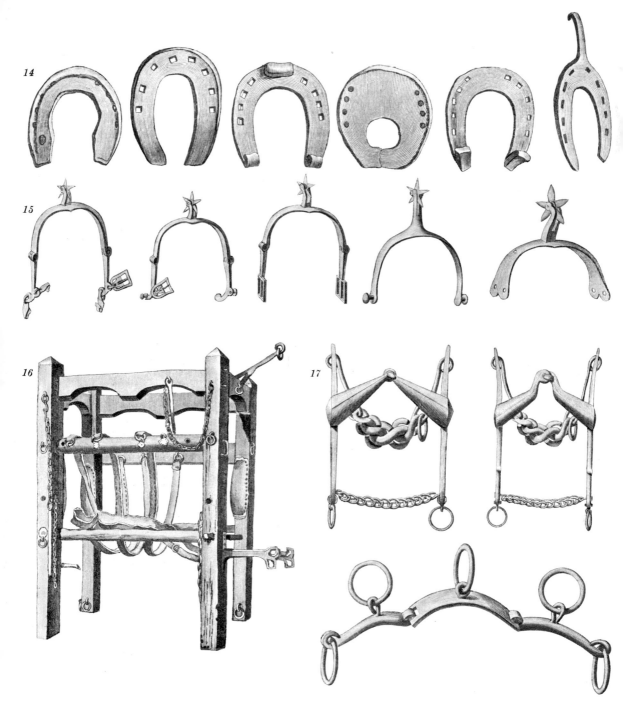

14

15

16   17

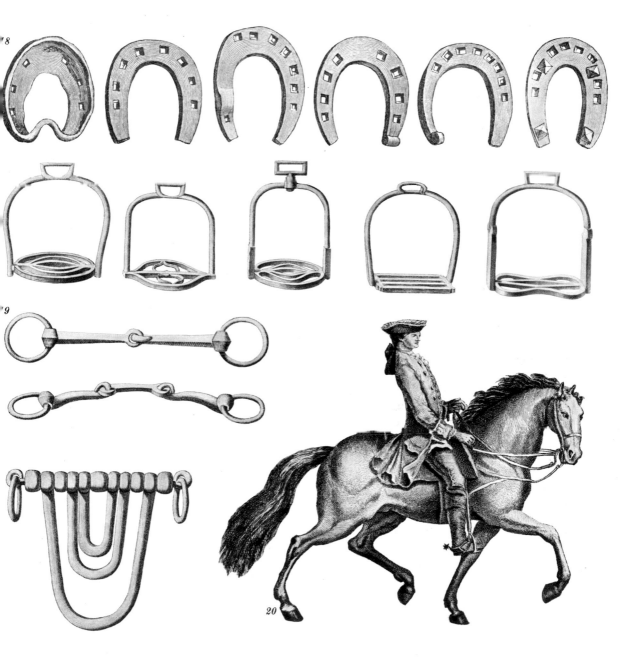

14-20 Horsemanship, from the gay 18th century cavalier below (20) to the training and management of coachhorses and heavy farm animals, became a complex and important business in the 18th and early 19th centuries. After that, with railroads and eventually automobiles, it gradually declined. The pictures on this page come from Diderot's famous "La Grande Encyclopédie," and include a group of horseshoes, both 18th century and ancient (14), typical 18th century spurs (15), stirrups (18) and bits (17 and 19), and a contraption (16) used for doctoring wounded horses.

20

the early Middle Ages, of an efficient method of harnessing a horse to a vehicle. This revolutionary discovery, which incidentally seems to have originated among the peoples of Central Asia, allowed the horse to exert his full strength without strangling himself in the process. The results were astonishing, for after the twelfth century there was a phenomenal increase in wheeled transport throughout Europe.

The horse could now pull in comfort, but the late medieval carriage itself was still little more than a heavy cart which could travel at no more than a walking pace and was incapable of a sharp turn. It was a great improvement, however, over the litters and carts of earlier years, and even women began to use it, especially of course ladies of noble or royal blood. Beatrice of Anjou, making her entrance into Naples in a small carriage lined with blue velvet in a pattern of golden lilies, or Isabeau of Bavaria, Queen of France, riding through Paris at the turn of the fifteenth century in a gaily painted vehicle, were much admired. In 1445 Marguerite of Anjou was proffered a similar vehicle by Henry VI of France.

Such ostentation among ladies of noble lineage aroused envy and emulation among their bourgeois counterparts—the wives and daughters of rich merchants and officials. In 1294 Philip the Fair forbade bourgeois women the use of the carriage. Not until 200 years later did the King of France for the first time allow the wife of the first President of Parliament, Christophe de Thou, to use the jolting carriage which her gouty husband had just acquired.

The medieval carriage was actually called just that, a "chariot branlant," or "jolting carriage." Its body was supported by chains, later by straps. Of Hungarian origin, the carriage for a long time was a rare sight, except perhaps in the cities, because there were few roads for it to use. Even in Paris there were only three in 1550, belonging respectively to Catherine de Medicis, to Diane de Montmorency, and to Jean de Laval. The first carriage appeared in London in 1555. Yet already one could discern in this crude vehicle the lineaments of the familiar carriage and stagecoach of later centuries.

But without adequate roads the vehicle had little chance to develop. As late as the seventeenth century, roads in Europe were very poor. Generally, they were used as a last resort, travel by water being much preferred. Medieval roads were really paths, almost trails. A slow improvement began first in France, which finally achieved a road system which was considered, until the days of McAdam, the finest in Europe. In 1559 Henri IV named Sully "Grand Voyer" of France, but the country had to wait until 1670 for the energetic Colbert to take definite measures, giving imperative instructions for the enlargement and upkeep of the French roade system.

In 1716 a Bridge and Pavement Office, which had recently been created, continued the work of reorganizing the French road system. This new body came up with the idea that all the roads should be laid out in a straight line. Despite this impractical idea, Daniel Trudaine, General Road Administrator in 1737, the engineer Jean Perronet, who in 1747 became head of the Ecole des Ponts et Chaussées, and others did some excellent work, building

21-23 Three 18th century prints show traditional Chinese transport: a farmer's cart (top), a sledge, and a noblewoman's closed carriage. Chinese vehicles like these date from ancient times, persist today.

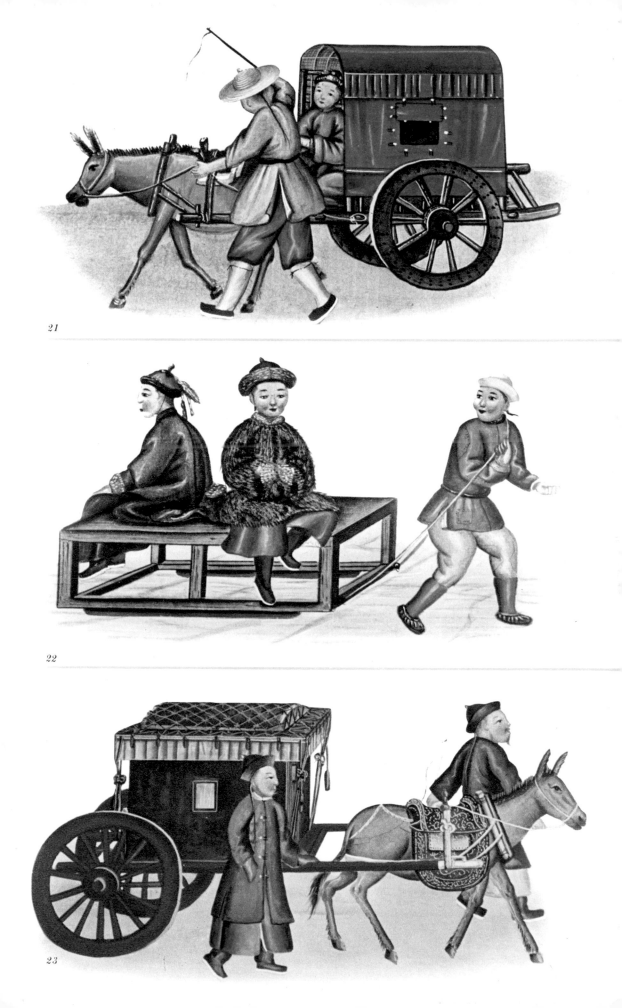

21

22

23

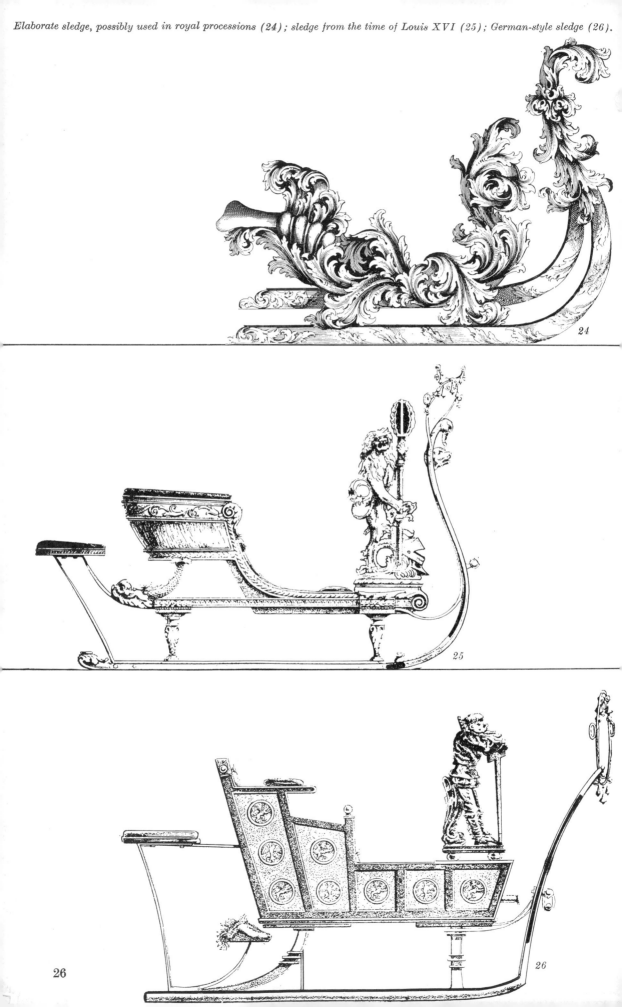

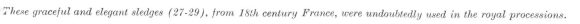
These graceful and elegant sledges (27-29), from 18th century France, were undoubtedly used in the royal processions.

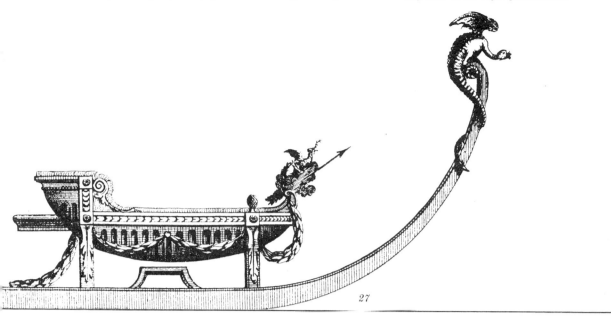

27

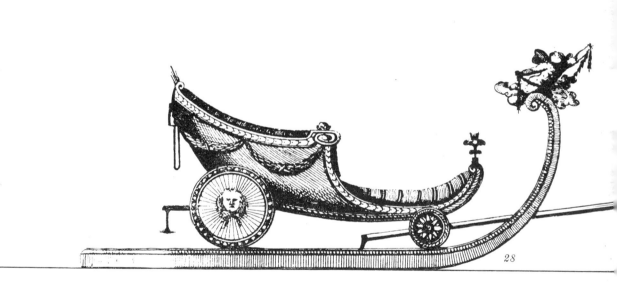

28

29

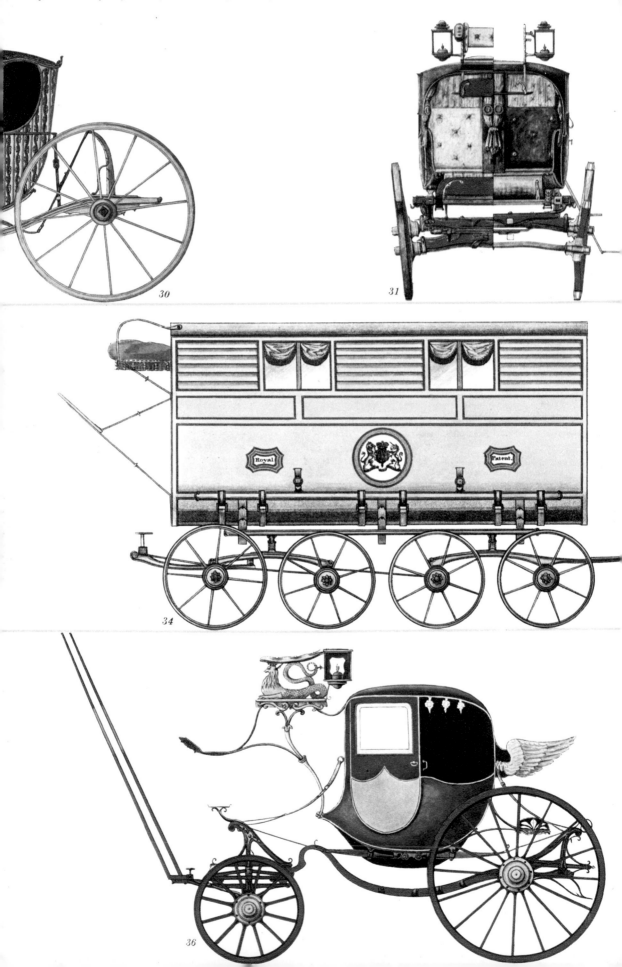

Early 18th century stagecoach (30); cut-away drawings of late 18th century carriage, front, side, and rear (31-33), both French.

32 33

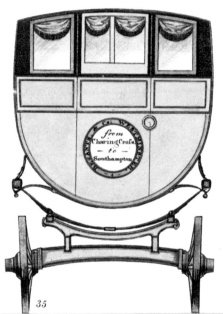

35

37

French vehicles of the 18th century, as shown in Diderot's Encyclopédie: post-chaise (38); calash (39); stagecoach (40).

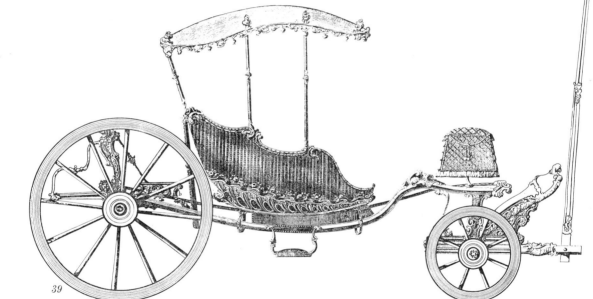

Three carriages of 18th century France: a light berlin (41); a four-door berlin (42); and Louis XVI's coronation coach (43).

41

42

43

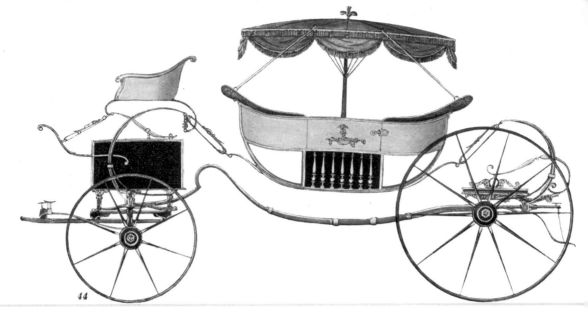

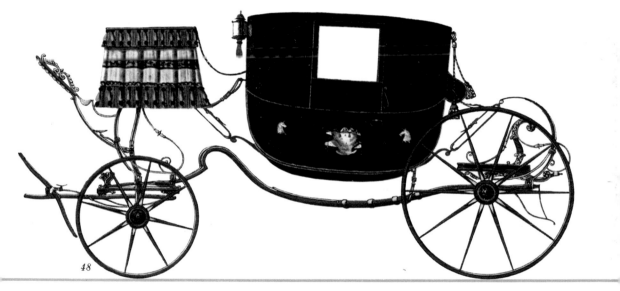

Elegant Duchesne "karick" of 1808 (51), and a "charrette" (50) and buggy (52) of 1907 show little change in almost a century.

Early twentieth century vehicles : the delicate Spider (53) ; an English "charrette" (54) ; and a phaeton for the ladies (55).

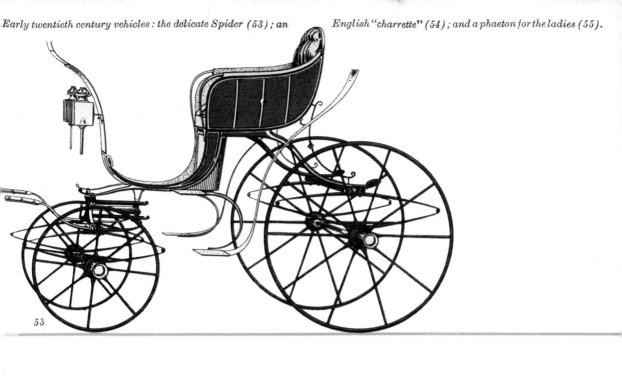

53

54

55

New York fire engines: "Old Maid," 1820s (56), had keg for "spirits"; "Black Joke," 1824 (57); and "Blue Boys," 1853 (58).

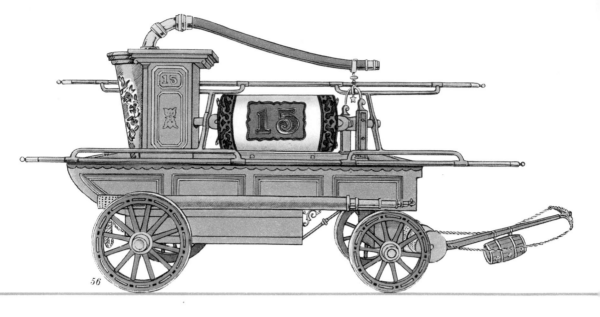

56

57

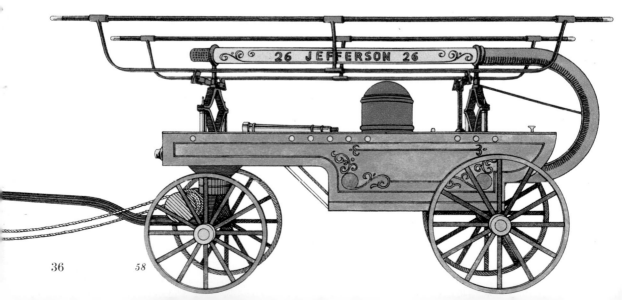

36   *58*

"Silver Nine," 1855 (59); "White Ghost," 1856 (60); "Elephant," 1859 (61), one of New York's first steam fire engines.

Commercial vehicles at the turn of the nineteenth century: a brewery wagon (62) and delivery wagons (63-64) with hooded seats.

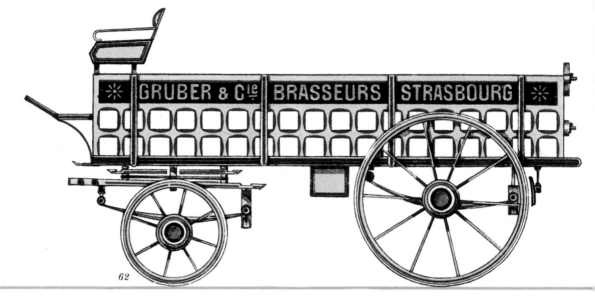

62

63

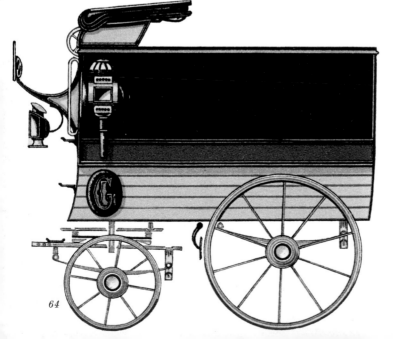

64

Wagons for delivery (note large lamps) (65-66), for transporting wine and liquors (67); and a cart with removable sides (68).

65

66

CAVES DU GRAND-HOTEL

COGNAC | MACON | MEDOC | RHUM

WHISKY | MARSALA | CHYPRE | LUNEL | MALAGA

67

68

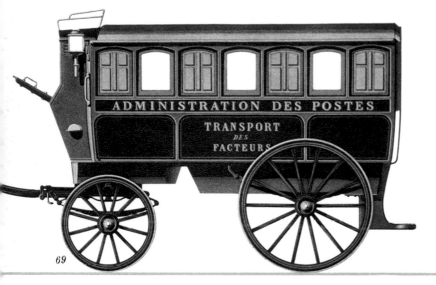

69

70

71

24,800 miles of roads. And their efforts continued. Philibert Trudaine, Daniel's son, and Turgot, who became minister in 1774, took up the torch. During the same period Pierre Trésaguet, who was Assistant General Inspector of Public Works in 1775, substituted for the massively constructed, dangerously bulging older roads a more rational type of construction with firm foundations and a solid layer of crushed stone on top.

And the other countries of Europe? Germany, fragmented into many small states, was greatly handicapped. Russia, lagging far behind European civilization, possessed very few roads except between the large cities. Italy was satisfied with her old Roman roads. Spain had to wait until the eighteenth century to see the beginnings of the great axis route from Madrid to the sea.

There remained England. For a long time her roads were no better than elsewhere. Then in 1815 the Scottish engineer, John Loudon McAdam, with a good deal of experience already behind him, undertook to repair the roads in the county of Bristol. Doing away with heavy foundations, he laid down a light mixture of broken stones, sand and water which proved so tough and resilient that the system, dubbed "macadam," soon spread throughout Europe.

Most bridges during the Middle Ages were made of wood. A few audacious builders worked with stone, but their audacity was not always rewarded, and many of their works simply collapsed—a misadventure which spared wood no more than stone. The Pont au Change in Paris met with this fate four times between the fifteenth and seventeenth centuries. Yet nothing discouraged the engineers. In a magnificent flourish, Antonio da Ponte spanned the Grand Canal of Venice with the Rialto Bridge in 1592—a single span of 84 feet supported on a veritable forest of piles. In 1769 Robert Mylne built the Blackfriars Bridge at London. Meanwhile Hans Grubermann had constructed the great Schaffhausen Bridge across the Rhine.

Gradually stone replaced wood, then was replaced in turn by iron—that is to say, cast iron. The first bridge to utilize this material was built to span the Severn in 1775 by the able English metal founder, Abraham Darby. He was followed by Thomas Telford, then by the Walkers. Frenchmen and Americans soon turned to iron bridges, and an American, James Finley, was the first to design and construct a true suspension bridge. This was in 1796.

We have strayed far from carriages and must return. The "chariot branlant" was replaced by the early stagecoach, which was something like a box mounted on four wheels, roomy and deep like an overturned "armoire," and scarcely more flexible. Certainly it was less proof against wind and rain. After the first wave of infatuation with the stagecoach, the inconveniences began to appear: jolts, dust, and drafts, which were so bothersome that people of quality were overjoyed when the marvellous Italian *caroccio* crossed the Alps and began to spread throughout Europe. This was the direct ancestor of the private carriage.

The first carriage, however, was a far cry from the elegant vehicle we usually think of when the term is mentioned. Nevertheless it

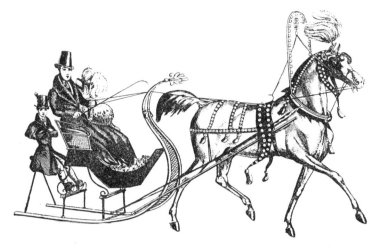

quickly became the mania of the aristocrats, then of the ministers, the lordlings, the clergy, and finally even the more astute of the bourgeoisie. And in time the crude wooden box, covered with cloth inside, turned into a veritable salon, richly decorated both inside and out. The "Grande Mademoiselle," niece of Louis XIII, for instance, showed herself at the "Cours la Reine" in a carriage with its leather "entirely covered with crimson red velvet, fastened with gold pins." As variety of taste is the rule in human nature, new types of carriages soon began to appear. In contrast to the rather massive aspect of the original carriage, which was a kind of heavy, gilded set-piece, there was the lightness of the calash, whose forward section was furnished with a leather apron or glass partition, while a leather hood could be raised or lowered over the seats. The calash, however, required six horses, the faster cabriolet only two. In Berlin Frederick William invented the berlin. It was very useful for travelling, but somewhat heavy. So it was cut in two and became the coupé.

It was the English above all who perfected the carriage, constantly increasing its lightness and flexibility. The superb British carriage-makers created an immense variety of vehicles which dominated the European market: tilburies, carricks, wiskis and others. English carriages, however, or imitations thereof, were generally confined to the richer nations.

With this profusion of carriages, everyone wanted to ride instead of walk. For those of modest means a public transportation system was created in eighteenth century France which,

because of its speed, was known as "the diligence"—six days instead of 18 from Paris to Lyons. Turgot's "turgotines," again, after 1775, were so much faster than the "diligence" that he was accused of ruining the inns of France, and also of atheism because he prevented Christians from hearing mass.

Thus the stagecoach gradually increased its speed. In the seventeenth century almost a month was required to travel from Paris to Toulouse; a hundred years later the time had been cut in half. Here again the English travelled faster and in greater comfort because their road system was being improved from day to day—eventually it was to become the best in Europe. English roads were positively humming with coaches, and as a result the average traveller began to fear for his life. One is reminded of Madame de Sevigné's cry, "I trust my daughter to you, don't overturn her..." And in a later period Victor Hugo's "What a horrible thing to spend a night in a mail coach!"

As for the city, the first taxis of Paris were no doubt those of the Marquis de Montbrun, who in 1639 made his sedan chairs available to the public. Soon afterwards Nicolas Sauvage, a former coachman, began to rent carriages complete with horses and driver. Since he placed himself under the protection of St. Fiacre his vehicles were popularly called "fiacres." Later on an idea of Pascal's led, in 1662, to the first omnibus line with a fixed route. These "carrosses à cinq sols"(the price of the trip) did not last long and were succeeded by Baudry's famous "Dames Blanches." Not until 1828, however, was Paris to see regular fleets of public

72   Very graceful sleigh used in Paris toward the end of the 19th century. Tiny rear seat may have been for a page or for a child. The horse's harness is in the Russian style.

transports—the "Favorites," the "Citadines," the "Batignollaises," the "Hirondelles," and many others.

On the other side of the Atlantic the story was much the same. The wheel was introduced to America by the colonists. The Indians used nothing but the "travois"—a species of sledge —or their legs; though with the latter they could cover as much as 76 miles in a day. In 1639 a road, probably the first, was laid out between Plymouth and Boston. In 1766, over a hundred years later, the "Flying Machine," a simple four-wheeled carriage drawn by four horses, still took over a day and a half to go from New York to Philadelphia. About the middle of the eighteenth century the celebrated Conestoga wagon made its first appearance. This huge, lumbering affair with four wooden wheels and a white canvas covering became the instrument, and at the same time the symbol, of the pioneers' penetration of the vast, uncharted reaches of America's heartland. Men walked at its side while women and children travelled within. Known familiarly as the "prairie schooner," the Conestoga wagon took part in all the major advances into the West, from the colonization of the Midwest to the discovery of gold in California. In 1813 the sturdy Concord stagecoach, capable of travelling a hundred miles in a day, made its appearance. In 1825 an enterprising New Yorker named Abraham Brower launched the first regular passenger service in the growing city. His "Accomodation" ran from Wall Street along Broadway to Bleecker Street. To stop the bus passengers had to yank a cord attached to the leg of the driver.

Around 1830 Americans east of the Mississippi, lured by tales of the rich lands to the west, began an unparalleled mass migration across hostile plains, deserts, and mountains. Their wagons followed two main routes: in the north the Oregon Trail along the Platte to Oregon, and in the south the Santa Fe Trail from St. Louis to Independence, Missouri and so to Santa Fe. The best wagons were turned out by the Studebaker brothers, who during the Civil War supplied them to the armies by the thousands for use as ambulances, shelters, and kitchens. As for New York City, by 1840 traffic had become so congested that it was dangerous for a pedestrian to cross the street. A decade later plans were developed for building footbridges and elevated sidewalks for his protection; but nothing came of it, and following the example of the capitals of Europe, the pedestrian, even as in our day, was left to his dangerous fate.

Meanwhile steam power had quietly made its first unpretentious appearance. Its origin was obscure, its growth a matter of convenience, like the gradual adoption of a rational way to harness a horse in the Middle Ages. The first steam engine was supposed to be that of Hero of Alexandria some 2,000 years ago. It consisted of a sphere spun around by two jets of steam escaping from bent tubes. But this served no useful purpose. Denis Papin, of France, seems to have proposed the first real steam engine in 1690. Because of steam, the horse-drawn carriage eventually disappeared, yielding to the railway and the automobile—and along with them a few oddities like the bicycle.

73   *A 19th century drawing shows a*
"sailing cart" careening smartly
down the tracks. Except for
iceboats, land vehicles with sails
have never been successful.

Take a cylinder containing water and closed by a piston. Heat it, and the steam raises the piston. Let it cool. The steam turns back into water, and as a result of atmospheric pressure the piston comes down again. Heat it, cool it, heat it, cool it... the piston will continue to work without fail.

This, more or less, was the way Denis Papin described his steam engine in his report of 1690 on "A new method of obtaining a great supply of power at low cost."

After Papin the initiative moved to the English. In 1698 Thomas Savery patented a simple steam pump, and in 1712 Thomas Newcomen and John Calley made another for use in the mines. In 1769 James Watt patented the first practical steam engine for sawmills, rolling mills, looms or anything else. After Watt the steam was condensed outside the cylinder and acted successively on both sides of the piston.

All that was left was to marry steam to the wheel. But at first the marriage gave birth to monsters. In 1769 Nicolas Cugnot launched his lumbering "fardier." On the other side of the Channel William Murdock experimented with a Watt engine, while in the United States Oliver Evans invented his steam carriage. Rails had been used for many years in the mines to carry dump trucks, and all of the earliest railroads were operated by a combination of horse- or mule-power and gravity. The first roadway built of rails in the United States, for instance, was a short track of wooden rails laid down about 1795 to transport crushed rock and cement to and from kilns on Beacon Hill in Boston. The first actual steam locomotive,

built expressly for rails, was operated by Richard Trevithick in England in 1804. "Yesterday," he wrote, "we made our first trip with the machine. We hauled ten tons of iron, five wagons, and 70 men." This first locomotive was slow, making only nine and a half miles in four hours. Another Trevithick engine, called "Catch Me Who Can," was exhibited in London in 1808 on a circular track near Euston Square surrounded by a fence. It was a kind of new-fangled merry-go-round, and was briefly successful because of its novelty. But soon Trevithick's resources were exhausted and he had to close down. As a locomotive Trevithick's machine was mistrusted, because everyone was convinced that the wheels would skid on the slippery rails if the load were increased.

Everyone was convinced, that is, except William Hedley, who in 1813 was the first to prove, by demonstration, that metal on metal alone would do for any load. He built three locomotives, of which one, "Puffing Billy," can still be seen at London.

George Stephenson was another exception, and an important one; for Stephenson above all others dominated the earliest years of the steam railroad. For twelve years he struggled almost alone with every aspect of the new invention, and in the end he was successful in everything he did. After repairing many locomotives and building others, he was at last able in 1825 to launch the first railway line specifically designed for passenger service as well as the hauling of coal. On September 27 his "Locomotion No. 1" pulled no less than 600 passengers over the 21 miles which separated Stockton from Darlington. An orchestra played and a horseman with a red flag rode at the head of the train—for security. Here was the real beginning of the railway.

In 1829 a line was planned between Liverpool and Manchester. The backers, hesitating between horses and locomotives, finally put up a £500 prize for the best locomotive available, and in the Rainhill trials Stephenson's engine, "The Rocket," was chosen. Equipped with a tubular boiler recently perfected by the French inventor, Marc Seguin, it hauled a 13-ton load at more than 15 miles per hour over the 63-mile stretch. According to the *Liverpool Courier* some 10,000 to 15,000 spectators watched the trials. "There has probably never been a similar occasion," it wrote, "which brought together so many scientists and engineers as yesterday on the railway."

The English press, referring to the Rainhill trials, spoke of "a demonstration whose results could change the entire system of our internal communications." It could not have been better stated. Great Britain continued to move forward, developing railways in her own country and then, thanks to such men as Robert Stephenson, son of George, and Isambard Brunel, exporting them to other countries throughout the world.

After 1830 small lines sprang up in England like mushrooms. These were followed by the trunk lines. The London-Birmingham line was opened in 1838. Then came the London-Newcastle, the London-Edinburgh and the London-Bristol.

Robert Stephenson not only continued to improve his locomotives but, following in his

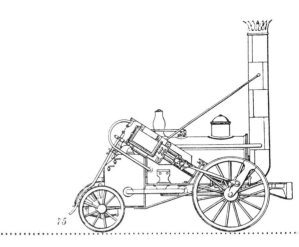

father's footsteps, he methodically attacked the problem of the infrastructure: clearance, ballast, and the laying of rails. He was also commissioned to lay out many railway lines in England and abroad. The longer lines often ran into difficulties. To connect London with Bristol, Brunel had to dig a tunnel almost two miles long, whereas Stephenson faced the old problem of bridges. He built the iron bridges of Newcastle-on-Tyne, of Berwick-on-Tweed, and the Britannia, which linked London with Wales over the Menai Straits. As early as 1840, as a result of such efforts, England could boast 76 railroad companies, including the celebrated Great Western of Bristol, and 2,235 miles of tracks.

Stimulated by Britain's progress, other countries began to show an interest in railroads. In 1833 the Belgian, Pierre Simons, developed plans for a network to cover his country, but again it was Robert Stephenson who built the first line, from Brussels to Malines. On its opening in 1835 the French journalist, Nisard, wrote: "A bell signalled the departure. Then the engine began to move, at first very slowly. But soon it came to life, and flew away as though trying to escape the noise of the wagon it was dragging behind it." In 1835, again, the Nuremberg-Furth line was opened in Germany with an Adler locomotive furnished by the peripatetic Stephenson. In 1830 the Reuse-Tarragona line was opened in Spain, in 1837 the Saint Petersburg-Tsarskoe Selo in Russia. The Milan-Monza line was opened in Italy in 1840 and in 1852 the Swiss Geneva-Zurich line.

Also in 1835, the French deputies were discussing a suggestion by Marc Seguin for a line from Paris to Saint-Germain. Some great men said some very foolish things. They persisted in thinking that the wheels would skid, not roll, and Arago seriously predicted that the tunnels would suffocate the passengers and give them pleurisy. Nevertheless, the line was built in 1837 and inaugurated by Queen Marie-Amélie and Princess Marie d'Orléans. It was a great success despite the stifled fears of the first passengers. In 20 days the train carried 400,000 passengers. Formerly it would have taken a year to transport the same number the same distance. The Paris-Rouen line followed; but resistance continued. "A railway running through Nancy will be harmful to the city's industry. Our factories have nothing to gain by the establishment of a railway..." No wonder France, with less than 2,484 miles of track in 1850, was in fourth place behind Germany with its 3,726 miles of track, England with its 6,521 miles, and the United States with 9,283.

It did not take long for the United States to capture the lead. For in America the railway was to discover its true vocation—to advance civilization by enabling man to weave a fruitful web over the immense and unproductive areas of the land. Those Americans who understood this had their work cut out for them; for New York on the Atlantic coast and San Francisco on the Pacific lay more than 3,000 miles apart. Compared to such distances, Paris to Berlin was a stroll, and Paris to Moscow merely a modest outing.

The American counterpart of George Stephenson was Colonel John Stevens, a distinguished inventor and engineer who as early

74 John Blenkinsop's early cog wheel locomotive, built in 1810.
75 George Stephenson's famous "Rocket." In 1829 it hauled 13 tons at nearly 16 miles per hour.

as 1811 petitioned the New Jersey legislature for a charter to construct a railroad, and in 1812 sought Congress's support for a national railroad. In 1825 he built a little steam locomotive at his own expense and ran it successfully around a circular track at his Hoboken, New Jersey estate. Although it was only a demonstration model, this was actually the first steam locomotive to run on rails in the United States.

In 1829 the Baltimore and Ohio, America's first great line, was opened, and for it Peter Cooper built his "Tom Thumb," the first operative American locomotive. Imported English locomotives had already proved too heavy for the lighter American tracks. In 1831 Phineas Davis's "Atlantic" won the Baltimore and Ohio $400 prize, while Baldwin's "Old Ironsides" made its first trip in 1832.

The descendants of these locomotives crossed the prairies, defied the deserts, withstood Indian attacks and train robberies, and conquered a land. With their broad "cow catchers" in front, their huge smokestacks, their ponderous and noisy bells, they pushed relentlessly forward, and wherever they went across the western country banks, saloons, churches and shops sprang up as if by magic. This was the heroic period of American railroading. But the most difficult task was to link the two oceans despite deserts and the Rocky Mountains. In 1858 the Central Pacific Company was chartered to build eastward from California, and in 1862 the Union Pacific to build west from Missouri. Finally on May 10, 1869 a golden spike marked the linking of the rails from East and West. At Promontory Point, Utah, the

"Jupiter" of the Central Pacific and the "119" of the Union Pacific confronted each other. The oceans had been joined.

For Americans, with their huge country, to travel further and faster was certainly important; but perhaps because they had known hard times in the beginning and because they had been poor, they valued comfort even more than speed. In this area one name stands out. George M. Pullman was determined to make a palace out of the train. In 1865 his luxurious "Pioneer" appeared. With its black walnut woodwork and rich Brussels carpets it provided the comfort of a first class hotel—and since the finest coal was used there was little odor of smoke. Pullman had democratized the luxuries already available to several sovereigns. Napoleon III, for instance, owned a train of nine inter-communicating carriages, built for him by the Compagnie des Chemins de Fer de l'Est, which included a dining car, an observation car, a salon, and a sleeping car.

After the middle of the century the train had come of age, for it had reached a speed of 62 miles (100 kilometers) per hour. As early as 1840 Daniel Gooch in England had realized that more speed could be obtained by increasing the size of the boiler and of the driving wheels. His ideas were taken up by Thomas Crampton; but the "Crampton" was adopted first on the continent: in 1848 on the Namur-Liège line and in 1849 on the Paris-Calais. These first "express trains" went as fast as 75 miles per hour; but they also began to carry an increasingly heavy load, which brought up again the old problem of wheel adherence. The

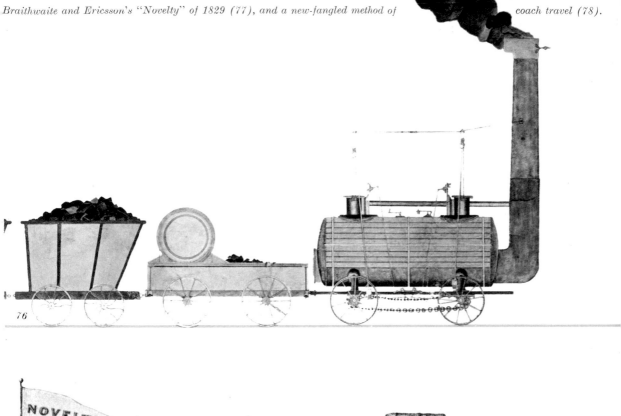

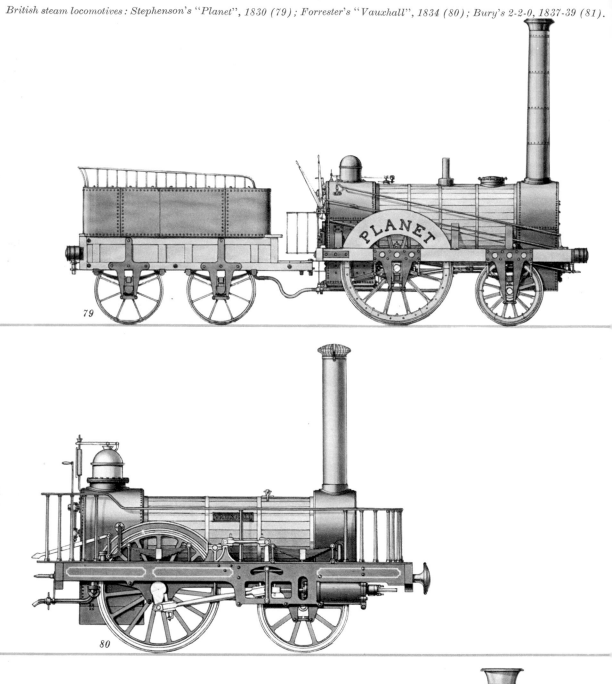

79

80

81

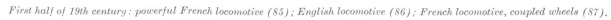

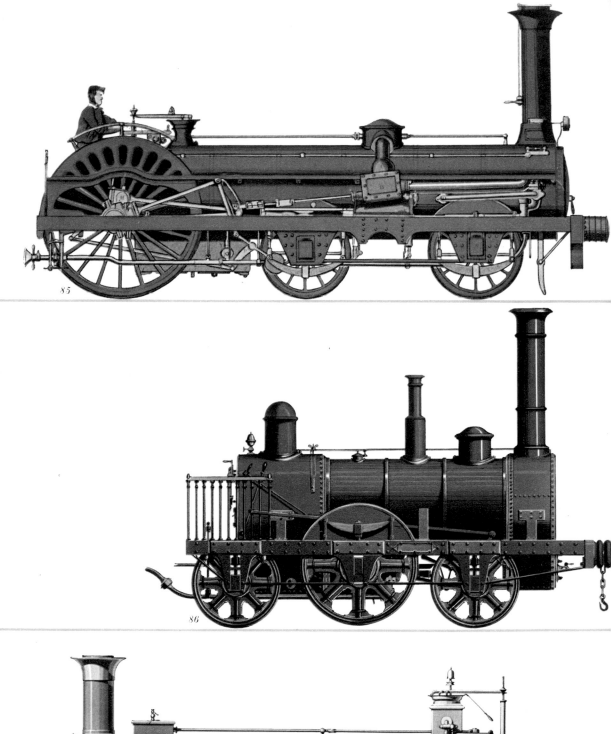

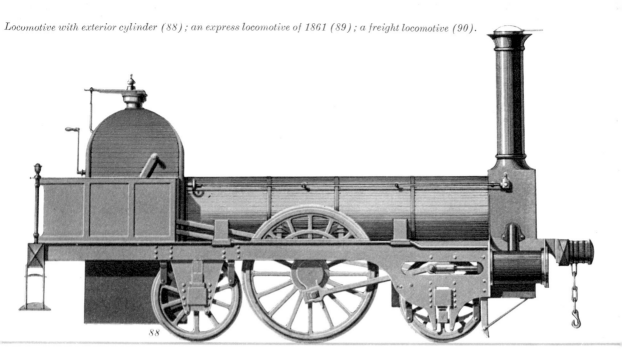

French railroad carriages, around 1910: first class passenger coach (91); third class coach (92); postal carriage (93).

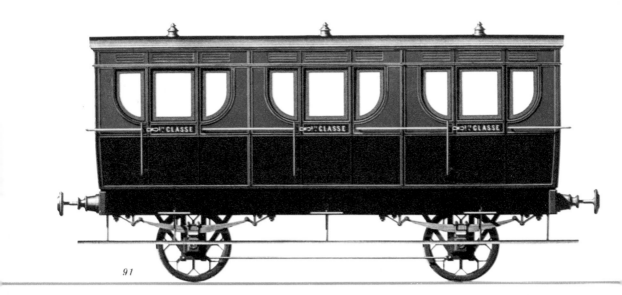

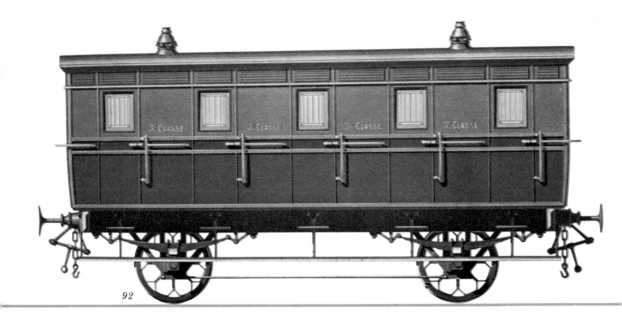

Late 19th century horse-drawn trams : the first Stephenson carriage brought to France, 1872 (94) ; two Parisian trams (95-96).

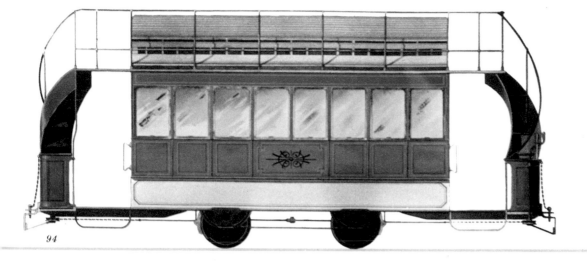

94

95

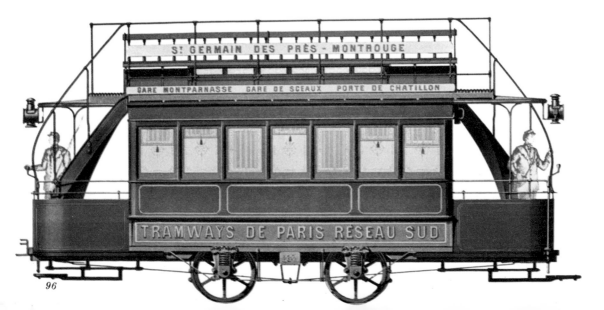

96

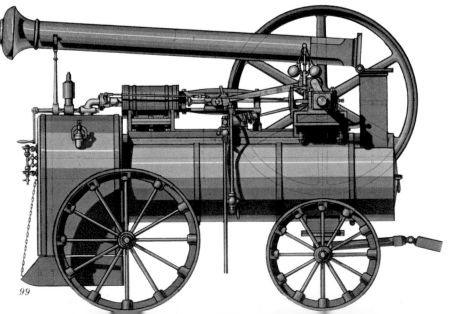

answer was found in coupled driving wheels. The "Farquenot" of 1864 developed 800 horsepower and weighed 35 tons; the "Outrance" of 1876 developed 1,200 horsepower and weighed 40 tons.

The modern locomotive was shaped by three new developments. First, the coupling of a high pressure and a low pressure cylinder to limit power waste. This was the compound engine, which was first tested by the Swiss, Mallet, on a small local railway between Bayonne and Biarritz. The French remained sceptical until the idea had been successfully proved out by an Englishman, Francis Webb, after which the French began buying and copying the Webb system. Next came superheating of the steam to a temperature of 200° to 300°, an idea which was successfully tested by a German, Wilhelm Schmidt, as early as 1891. And finally, with increased speeds, improved brakes were a necessity. In 1868 the American George Westinghouse invented the air brake to replace the cumbersome handbrake. Henceforth a single motion by one man could stop any train.

By the end of the nineteenth century both the design and the construction of the conventional mainline steam locomotive had become relatively stabilized. It had reached the maximum size that a fireman could fire by hand—about 5,000 pounds of coal per hour (for coal, rather than wood as in the earlier locomotives, was now the common fuel). This in turn limited the continuous locomotive output to about 1,500 horsepower, so that around the turn of the century locomotive designers, faced with the need to haul heavy

freight trains, strove for the maximum tractive effort at low speeds rather than an increase in horsepower.

Nevertheless, before the mainline steam locomotive disappeared from the rails, horsepower, and tonnages too, climbed still higher —from 1,500 horsepower to 3,000 and above. In sheer weight and power the Americans, with their wide open spaces, excelled. The "Niagara" weighed 225 tons, while the colossal Mallet-type articulated locomotive weighed 285 tons. As for speed, in 1936 a German engine reached an experimental speed of 124 miles per hour. Where was Hedley's little "Puffing Billy" with its four miles per hour?

As the railroads spread around the world, varying climates and needs produced new adaptations. There were the long lines, such as Africa's "Cape to Cairo Railway" built by Cecil Rhodes. In Abyssinia the French line of Addis Ababa, which entered into competition with the caravans well before 1900, boasted a record 12 tunnels and 92 bridges or viaducts along its 310 miles. South Africa has the reputation of possessing one of the most remarkable rail networks in the world. In Natal province, for instance, special locomotives were built to climb the grades, which reach a height of 6,562 feet.

Electricity and aerodynamics have, of course, brought about the greatest adaptations in modern railroading—but first, a few curious and even fantastic types of railroad. There is the atmospheric railway, for instance, the idea of which is to force a piston through a tube by creating a vacuum, and then attach the train to the piston. In Ireland, land of dreams,

100 Comfort was the proud
boast of the American railroads
towards the end of the 19th
century. This poster conveniently
combines a suggestive pose with
a route map of the railroad.
101 French switchman of 1890.
102 Pullman cars of the late
19th century provided travel
comfort, ornate interiors.

Clegg and Samuda actually constructed an atmospheric railway between Kingstown and Dalkey in 1843. This worked—but in a manner far from regular. Even France, despite her success with more conventional types for railroad, experimented with an atmospheric system at the end of the Saint-Germain line in 1847. It was a total failure. Around 1830 an Englishman named Brown tested a gas locomotive. But the wind was cheaper, and easily available, and there were many attempts, most of them quite serious, to work out a sail-train on tracks. In 1829 and 1830 the South Carolina Railway tried out a sail-equipped wagon which carried 15 passengers between Charleston and Hamburg. Much later, and far more successfully, the Kansas Pacific Railroad used a small sail car for many years along sections of track on the western plains to carry its railroad repairmen from place to place. With a good wind, it could travel as fast as an express.

Finally, there was the wild (and, who knows, perhaps humorous idea) of the two Englishmen who in 1845 established a "caniposte" railway to carry fish between Blankenberghe and Bruges in Belgium. Every detail had been foreseen: "Four dogs are attached to a light carriage carrying two tons of fish. Famished with hunger, they are induced to run by a piece of fresh meat suspended a few inches from their noses. For faster postal transportation, two greyhounds are to be attached. Instead of a piece of meat, a dead or a stuffed hare will be suspended from a rod on the carriage, which will appear to be running away from the starved dogs."

103   *The velocipede, with one huge wheel in
front and a tiny one behind, was all the rage
in the middle of the 19th century. Since it was
dangerous and difficult to ride, the velocipede
was favored by gay young blades like these.*

The two greatest means of land transportation are undoubtedly the railway and the automobile. In so far as land space and human needs are concerned, these two are certainly the most widespread and the most vital. Yet as man travelled about the world he was often forced to solve problems in transportation which called for something different.

Of these lesser forms of land transportation, the bicycle has always been the favorite. From birth it was assured of a brilliant future. Originally a fashionable novelty, a luxury toy for gilded youth, the bicycle through a strange turning of fate became the most economical and for a time one of the most popular means of transportation.

The ancestors of the bicycle, or two-wheeler, date far back into history. In Egyptian art, for example, a small device is shown which seems to have two wheels connected by a bar. The Chinese knew a similar device, but it had bamboo wheels. Centuries later we find a recognizable bicycle among the designs in Leonardo da Vinci's inexhaustible notebooks.

The history of the two-wheeler really began in Paris around 1790 when the "célérifère," also known as the "horse on wheels," appeared. Possibly invented by the eccentric Count of Sivrac, it consisted of a wooden body mounted on two wheels, and carrying the head of a lion, dragon or stag at one end. It could not be steered and was operated by the feet, and was an extremely rigid device which, considering the roads of the time, must have been hard on the rider's constitution. Nevertheless, no sooner had it appeared under the green chestnut trees of the Champs-Elysées than it

104

105

104   The "draisine," shown here
in a form which closely resembles
the original patent drawings, was
invented by Drais von Sauerbronn
of Baden-Baden and patented
in 1817. In a matter of years
after its invention this ancestor
of the bicycle became tremendously
popular, first in France, then
in England and the United States.
It was also called the
"Hobbyhorse" or "dandyhorse"
and was often used by young bloods
for racing around circular
tracks or in indoor arenas.
105   A tricycle, with hand crank,
invented by Boadley in 1839.
106   An American monocycle,
patented around 1880 when the modern
bicycle was being perfected.

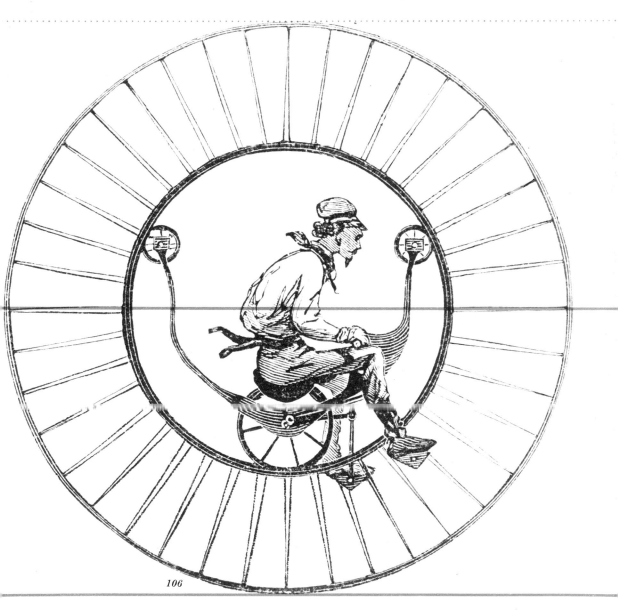

106

107-108 *Two Otto "Safety" bicycles, constructed by the Birmingham Small Arms Company in 1881 and (below) 1879. These cumbersome machines were closely related to the famous high bicycle of the period with its huge front wheel. The idea was to go as fast as possible without having to pedal too rapidly.*
109 *Bicycle suspension patented in 1890 by Dunlop, inventor of the pneumatic tire. High bicycles were outmoded after 1880 when pedals, sprocket and chain were placed between wheels.*

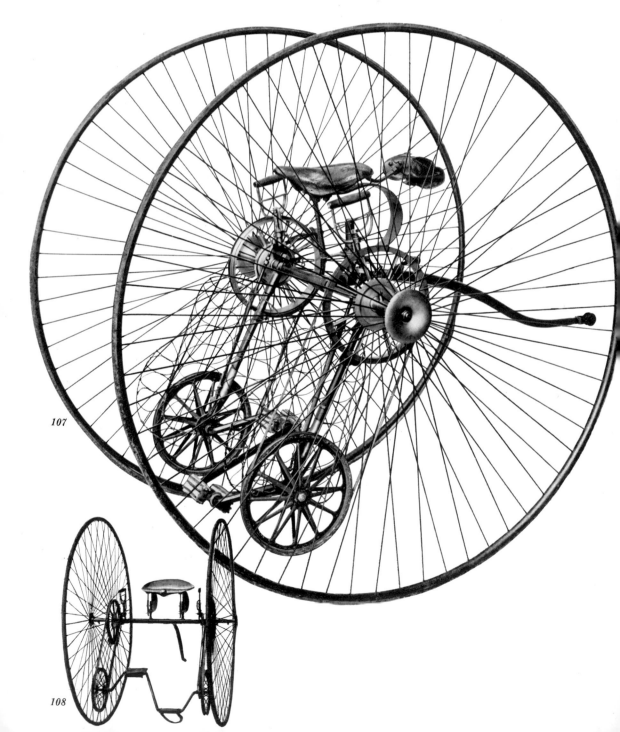

107

108

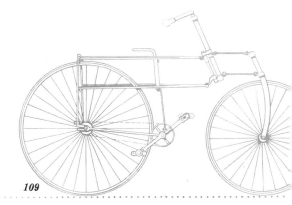

109

became a huge success, being immediately adopted by those dandies, the "Incroyables."

The "célérifère," increasingly popular during the French Directory and First Empire, soon became known as a "vélocifère" and began to leave the streets of Paris for the dusty country roads. It even crossed the Channel, where its success in England was equally astounding.

About 30 years after its invention the two-wheeler began to be accepted as a real means of transportation. It was Drais von Sauerbronn of Baden-Baden who effected this transformation by slipping some springs beneath the seat and then adding a handle bar to steer the front wheel, thus creating the famous "Draisine" of 1818. Its success was even greater than that of the already outmoded "célérifère." As early as 1819 the new device had crossed the Atlantic to conquer America. In New York, where it was called the "Dandy Horse," the Draisine amazed and delighted everyone, and the merchants made a fortune out of it. In Europe, meanwhile, the two-wheeler crowd, leaving the city, began to push along the roads at all of eight miles per hour, a speed which the pedestrians found alarming.

In 1839 a Scottish manufacturer, Kirkpatrick MacMillan, improved the Draisine by equipping it with a complex set of levers to drive the wheel. He should have gone on to discover the pedal, but failed to do so. One day as he was riding his machine down a hill he found himself unable to stop and ran over a child. Disgusted with what he had done, he abandoned his new device.

The pedal, which was invented by Pierre Michaux in 1861, completely revolutionized the two-wheeler industry, leading to a prodigious growth. Now called a "vélocipède," the new pedal machine became immediately fashionable and spread throughout Europe. Lallement, one of Michaux's workmen, went to the United States in order to convert the Americans to the new device.

In 1869, when the manufacturing of two-wheelers had already become an industry, the first race took place along an 80-mile route between Paris and Rouen. The race was won by an Englishman, James Moore, who covered the distance at an average speed of eight miles an hour. At almost the same time the wooden wheel was turned into a metal one. Then James Starley invented wire spokes. In 1875 Jules Truffaut first produced an inward-curving rim and afterwards gave it a rubber coating.

By this time the two-wheeler had become the pet of the people. All that was needed was a little money and some muscle, and one could ride to work, or escape on Sundays from the oppressive atmosphere of the big cities. The success of the velocipede also brought about a rediscovery of nature and of the open road. When spring arrived people rode out from the city, mounted on the "petite reine," for a picnic in the woods or beside some stream. The roads were generally deserted—except for the doctor's cabriolet or the peasant's cart—because most people now travelled by railroad. The two-wheeler was king of the road, and would remain so until the noisy invasion of the automobile in the twentieth century.

Acrobats, another category of velocipedists, also used the two-wheeler but in a decidedly different manner. In circuses, music halls, and

110

111

even public squares the subjects of Her Gracious Majesty Queen Victoria or of Napoleon III applauded the daring young riders who balanced on a cable stretched 75 feet above the ground. In the United States the Hanlon Brothers went on a grand tour with their velocipedes. It was so successful that on their return they established a school. Now anyone could become a velocipedist and be admired by the crowd, and for only $15.

People soon began to realize that if they enlarged the wheel to which the pedals were fastened, they could go faster without increasing the pedal strokes. This idea was first taken up by the British, and it was in their country that the bicycle known as the "Big Bi" was developed. It was a strange device, with an enormous wheel in front and a tiny one behind. The man—no woman could be got to ride it— sat in a saddle which almost touched the handle bar and was perched near the top of the big wheel. Since not everyone cared to climb so high, it was natural that a kind of snobbery of cycling grew up on both sides of the Atlantic. Bicycle fans banded together to form clubs. The most impressive club in the United States was the Bicycle Club of Boston.

An Englishman, Harry Lawson, thinking that there must be some way to ride at a decent speed without perching among the clouds, conceived the idea of placing the pedals between the two wheels, with a chain driving the rear one. After this invention the wheels promptly returned to their normal size, since henceforth the speed merely depended upon the size of the sprocket. It was now 1880, and the bicycle was born. It was still heavy, very

heavy, weighing about 80 pounds and was hardly comfortable; but improvements followed—a lighter frame, ball bearings, improved brakes, and the rubber tire.

The real inventor of the tire was an Englishman, Robert Thomson, who took out a patent in 1845; but his invention did not catch on and was soon forgotten. Many years later an Irish veterinary, John Boyd Dunlop, examining his little boy's tricycle, had the idea of fitting a rubber tube filled with air to the wheels to deaden the jolts. After initial experiments, he took out a patent for his invention as early as 1888. It was still a very crude tire which was glued directly to the rim after it was filled with air. Naturally, when a puncture occurred, hours were spent repairing it. Nevertheless, the Dunlop tire, which was to make bicycling practical, eventually became a great success.

In order to convince its many detractors of its worth, the tire had to be more easily removable. Fortunately the Michelin brothers of Clermont-Ferrand had worked out a removable tire; but for two long years (1888-1890) they tried, with no success, to win acceptance for their idea. They supplied their tire to Charles Terront for the memorable Paris-Brest race of 1891, but even he did not believe in it. But when he won the race with a lead of eight hours over the runner-up, despite five punctures during the course, he began to feel differently about this Michelin tire. There was something to it after all.

The grand result of Terront's victory can be summed up with brevity. In 1890 there were only 5,000 cyclists in France. In 1900, a decade later, there were ten million, which gives some

112

small idea of the intensity of the bicycle craze. And it was the same in the United States, Britain, and elsewhere. During the fad every kind of machine made its appearance: tricycles, small tricycles, carrier tricycles, tandem bikes, and even a bicycle built for five — a rather long machine, as one can imagine, with five men astride two wheels, their backs bent earnestly forward, maneuvering five sets of pedals all at once. So quickly did the bicycle develop that by 1911, on the eve of the First World War, it was already equipped with most of the improvements with which we are familiar today: the Bowden brake, a headlight fed by a small dynamo, and multiple speed gears.

The fad also brought forth many champions. In 1893, at the Buffalo Velodrome, the great Henri Desgranges lapped a course of 21 miles in one hour. Today Roger Rivière can do 32 miles in the same time. In 1928 a Belgian, Vanderstuyft, behind a motorcycle, broke another record by covering 80 miles in one hour. The Tour de France, first of the great national tours, was born in 1903, and was followed by the Giro d'Italia.

Cycling did not take long to spread throughout the world, and during the period between the two world wars it became a favored means of transportation. In factory towns, on a grey, cold dawn, workers and miners could be seen on the wet pavements on their way to work, a long thin line of cyclists, hunched into their saddles, their heads buried in their collars. But since the last war the bicycle has lost ground to that all-devouring monster, the automobile, as well as to the bus and tram. And to its cousins, the motorcycle, motorbike,

and scooter. Cycling is returning to what it was originally, a game (but this time for children), a sport, an entertainment, or sometimes a solitary pleasure.

The bicycle owes much of its popularity to the simplicity of its motor—in other words, muscle. But human muscle has very definite limits, and not everyone has the strong legs and good wind required for cycling. For the lazy and the weak—and for those who always wanted to go faster and faster—it was not long before the powerful motorized two-wheeler was created.

At the close of the Second Empire, in 1868, Pierre Michaux, father of the velocipede, worked out plans for a steam-powered bicycle. But somehow the idea did not seem very attractive and the inventor was the first to abandon it. Later on there was an attempt to equip the "Big Bi" with a piston engine, but this also met with failure. Although there were many other curious experiments, it was not until 1885 that what can be truly called the first motorcycle made its appearance—thanks to Daimler's original automobile engine.

The engine was placed within the frame of what appeared to be a cross between a bike with pedals and a primitive automobile, and it turned the rear wheel by means of a leather belt. But Daimler was more interested in the automobile proper, and his motorcycle idea was not taken seriously until the Werner brothers' machine appeared on the market in 1897. The Werner machine could do 24 miles per hour. Around 1902 it was followed by Knap's machine, which had its motor on the rear wheel. Soon thereafter the motorcycle

110   First steam-driven bicycle, 1870.
111   This 1887 paraffin vapor motor with
       five rotating cylinders was fixed to the
       front wheel of a tricycle in 1888.
112   Dion-Bouton gasoline tricycle, 1895.

113   *The first steam carriage was Frenchman Robert Cugnot's "Fardier."*
        Tested in 1769, it traveled at 2.5 miles per hour.

114   *Steam carriage built by English engineer William Symington in 1786.*

115   *Tested in London in 1803, the steam carriage of Richard Trevithick*
        and Andrew Vivian ran at a speed of 5-6.5 miles per hour.

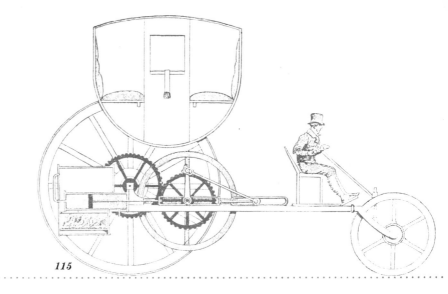

115

(long before the automobile) acquired its present shape and characteristics. By 1928 it already had its squat look, its easy driving, its lightning acceleration.

We must go back several years, to 1922, to find the beginnings of the scooter, another machine whose appearance has also been little changed. Although very practical and ingenious, the original motor scooter was not a success and was quickly forgotten. Then suddenly, after an eclipse of a quarter of a century, it was reborn after the war in Italy, and has since enjoyed an unprecedented success around the world. The Lambretta, the Vespa, and all their little brothers seem to symbolize for the pedestrian on the street as well as for their owners the slightly crazy, very noisy, but carefree exuberance of youth. It remains to be seen, however, whether the scooter will have the long and brilliant career of the delicate "petite reine."

There remain two transportation families which are as opposed, and as irreconcilable, as the Montagues and the Capulets—the one clean and white as snow, the other grimy with smoke and tar. First, there is the little family of urban transport. Towards the close of the eighteenth century the great capitals of Europe, London, Paris, Vienna, began to grow so rapidly under the impact of the industrial revolution that some form of urban transportation became an absolute necessity, for the teeming millions had no other means of getting about. At first private individuals, and finally the cities themselves filled the need. It will be remembered that the Marquis de Montbrun first had the idea of renting out his

sedan chairs, and that Nicolas Sauvage later made a very good living by supplying horse-drawn carriages for a fee. Thus was born the fiacre, the distant cousin of our taxi.

Since not everyone could afford to hire a fiacre, some less expensive means of transportation had to be found. For at least a century stagecoach lines had been running from city to city along the public roads. Why not organize similar public transportation companies within the cities? This was a simple idea which, moreover, appealed to Blaise Pascal. So it was largely due to a great philosopher that as early as 1662 the first "omnibus à cinq sols" began to circulate in Paris between the Porte St. Antoine and the Luxembourg. Unfortunately, since the line was forbidden to "pages, lackeys, and other liveried servants" it soon became unpopular and eventually was forgotten. Paris had to wait until 1828 to enjoy a regular service again. This was Baudry's horsedrawn "Dames Blanches," which ran from the Madeleine to the Bastille. They were a great success. Eight years later Paris had ten omnibus companies serving 53 lines and transporting more than 100,000 people a day.

The same thing happened in England and the United States. By 1830 New York, whose population had reached 200,000, found Bower's "Accomodations" and "Sociables" inadequate to the need. An enterprising banker, James Mason, was responsible for an important innovation, the horsedrawn tramway, which was worked out by the great Robert Stephenson. Thus in 1832 New York, and the world, saw its first "horsecar" running along the newly-paved Bowery. It was an overwhelming

116

success and was soon seen everywhere—New Orleans, Boston, Philadelphia, Paris in 1855, London a few years later. The cars were single or double-decked, sometimes open, sometimes closed. But in any case the new idea soon became indispensable to the life of the great modern city, and in a few years turned into the first generally accepted urban transportation system. In 1886 more than 100,000 horsecars were serving a half million lines in at least 300 different cities.

Nevertheless, while the number of passengers and cars continued to increase, horsepower remained the same that is, limited. People began to look to steam, and finally electricity, as a substitute, and plans began to be laid for running the tracks above or beneath the streets. The first underground railway was London's Metropolitan District Railway of 1863 with the novelty of gas-lighting in the carriages. Steam locomotives made life difficult for the passengers, but even so there were still ten million the first year. Paris did not start its "Métropolitain" until 1898, nor New York its subways until 1900. The Paris and New York systems were of course electrified from the start. But New York had had elevated railways since 1868, when the system was hailed as the answer to all its problems of congestion. The "elevateds," however, have now almost completely disappeared, and the underground subways have taken over.

The small electric train of Siemens and Halske, exhibited at the Berlin Exposition of 1879, and its successor, an electric tram line of 1881 built at Lichterfelde near Berlin, seem to have inaugurated the electric tramway, which quickly spread throughout Europe, then took hold in the United States in 1886, with Frank Sprague's line at Richmond, Virginia. The reign of the electric tram, or "trolley," was brief but glorious. In the cities, after a brief interlude in which cable-drawn trams were popular, it replaced the horsecars, then moved out into the country as the "interurban," a species of heavy tram which often went as fast as 80 miles per hour. In recent years, under pressure from the automobile and autobus, the tram has withdrawn again into the cities. It now seems to be going the way of the horse.

It was natural that our last little family, that of mountain transport, should have been born in Switzerland. In 1871 Nicholas Riggenbach opened the first rack-railway up the Rigi near Lucerne. Several years later the researches of the Swiss engineer Abt led to the invention of the funicular, or cable railway. But the slopes to conquer became increasingly steep and the cable railway was then supplemented by the téléferic, or elevated cable car, which as early as 1910 had been used in the quarries of Pennsylvania. It could go higher than all the other means of land transportation—if it could be called "land" transportation. The latest, that of the Aiguille du Midi at Chamonix, longest in the world, runs for 9,610 feet high above the peaks and glaciers.

There remains the monorail, a car running on a single rail. It seems like a useful idea, but has somehow never caught on. The Irish tested one in 1887, but succeeded in convincing no one of its value, not even themselves. In 1957 the Germans installed a monorail near Cologne which is still running.

116 *Painting showing steam-driven,*
three-wheeled stage coach which
Englishman W. Church intended to
put into service between London
and Birmingham. It was designed
for 22 passengers on the outside
and 22 more inside.
117 *"Steam carriage for common*
roads," patented in 1833 by John
Squire and Francis Macerone.
118 *Another version of Church's*
1833 steam carriage, this one to
have held 56 people. Tests of
this enormous and clumsy vehicle
were so disappointing that it was
never put into service.

117

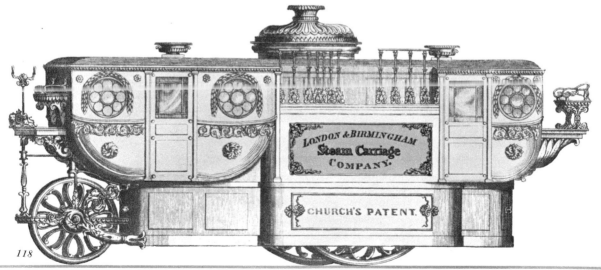

118

119 *Young ladies of Turin pass the time of day*
with a game called "diabolo" while the men
are devilishly busy trying to repair the car.
Frequent breakdowns in deserted country, bad
roads, and dust were all hazards of early motoring.

Throughout history the horse, pulling a vehicle, has been extremely useful to mankind; but man is not a grateful creature. As time went on he could think only of replacing the horse with an engine—any kind of an apparatus that would provide him with more energy to get from one place to another.

But before he was able to develop an engine whether steam, electricity, or gasoline—that would convert the usual conveyance into an automobile, man, curiously enough, turned back once more to himself. And so we come to those curious mechanical vehicles of the sixteenth and seventeenth centuries that were operated by hand levers. In 1645 Jean Théson was granted the right "to put into use a small, four-wheeled carriage driven without horses by two seated men, by himself invented." Another carriage, conceived around 1600 by a German, Hautsch, "goes forwards and backwards and turns without horses." Without horses, always without horses! It was an obsession, and it continued through the eighteenth century, except that the latest idea was to replace levers with pedals. In the end people realized that it was just as expensive to feed a man as a horse.

The wind, on the other hand, was free. The ancient Chinese had attached sails to their carts and wheelbarrows to help them along, and in Europe the Elector Johann Friedrich had built a vehicle of this type at Torgau in 1543. In 1600 Simon Stevin, a military engineer, built a famous chariot for Maurice of Nassau. It had two masts, a plough-shaped rudder, and all kinds of ingenious devices for trimming or lowering the sails with dispatch. An Englishman, George Pocock, launched a graceful,

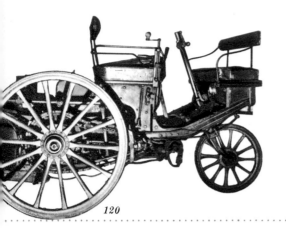

120

121

smaller carriage in 1826. This he called the "Flying Chariot." No horse, of course. Instead, it was pulled by a train of kites which seemed to lie indolently against the clouds. But yet it worked, for not only did its speed average from 15 to 20 miles an hour, but on one occasion Pocock's fragile phaeton enjoyed the luxury of passing the Duke of Gloucester's four-horse carriage.

Among other wind-propelled vehicles there was also the "flying coach" of the Spaniard, Don Jose Boscasa, and Hacquet's "Eolienne." The latter, favored by a southwest wind, actually sailed through the streets of Paris one day in 1834.

The first steam carriage which actually worked was Nicolas Cugnot's "fardier," a large, clumsy cart which could go no faster than four miles per hour. Intended to transport guns or other heavy loads, it was made of stout beams and had three huge, iron-strapped wheels, with power delivered direct to the single wheel in front by two massive cylinders. A big boiler and firebox were suspended over the front wheel, making it even more cumbersome. This frightening monster, which was tested before the Minister Choiseul in 1769, had to stop every 15 minutes to get up more steam, and vibrated so much that it finally escaped from its inventor and tore into a wall of the arsenal. Nevertheless, it was the first vehicle in which the thrust of pistons successfully turned a driving wheel; in other words it was really the first automobile.

The "fardier" can still be seen at the Conservatoire des Arts et Métiers in Paris. On view at the Birmingham Museum is the second forerunner of the automobile, a small steam model built by William Murdock, Watt's assistant, in 1784. With its light wheels and little smokestack at the back it looks frail compared to the heavy "fardier." The third pioneer vehicle was Oliver Evans' steam carriage, which he drove through the streets of Philadelphia toward the end of 1804. It was a huge amphibious boat which had been built to dredge the Schuylkill River. Evans named it the "Orukter Amphibolos," or the "digger which works all ways" because it was equipped with wheels for land travel and a paddlewheel for the water. And it actually worked, lumbering several miles over uneven ground before entering the river, where the paddlewheel took over from the belts which drove the wheels.

Encouraged by the success of Cugnot, Murdock, and Evans, others soon turned their hands to steam machines. In 1801 Richard Trevithick, helped by André Vivian, built a steam carriage with the engine in the rear which could carry about a dozen passengers at nine miles an hour. Two years later, before turning to the steam railway, Trevithick actually ran a steam tricycle through the streets of London. In the next 30 years or so quite a number of self-propelled steam carriages were built and operated on the new, hard-surfaced roads of England—and with considerable success. Outstanding was the steam carriage of Goldsworthy Gurney, which weighed two tons. By 1832 his coach was running on schedule four times daily between Gloucester and Cheltenham. In 396 trips it carried 3,000 passengers without mischance. Around 1834 Walter Hancock was operating several lines,

122

including his Paddington-City of London run. But eventually all these coaches disappeared, and the same thing happened in France—even though Onésiphore Pecqueur in 1828 had invented true modern steering with two wheels, and the differential for a rear-wheel drive.

But it is easy to understand the reason for the repeated failures of these steam coaches. It was the railway, of course. It could go faster with greater safety and economy, while at the same time carrying more passengers and hauling more freight. The success of the train was irresistible and universal; it dominated everything. Naturally the steam coachmen were hostile to it and even resorted to sabotage when necessary; but in the end the railroad interests—combined with owners of horse-drawn stages, with people who sold horses, with turnpike companies, and farmers who grew oats for fodder—pushed through a series of laws hampering and taxing the road locomotives, forbidding them to travel faster than four miles an hour, and finally requiring a man with a red flag to precede each self-propelled vehicle on a public highway. The latter act was not repealed until 1896. Thus with the failure of the steam coaches Britain was deprived of any chance for an early lead in the automobile field.

Despite such discouragements, despite the ever-greater success of the all-devouring railroad, despite everything, the steam automobile enthusiasts refused to surrender. It was the Bollées, father and sons, who brought steam back onto the roads. Their first machine was the "Obéissante," a 15-horsepower monster weighing five tons and travelling at 24 miles per hour. It was well received when it was shown in Paris in 1873. Five years later the "Mancelle," a much smaller machine, made its appearance. It was much more economical to operate. By this time the Bollée machines began to be known throughout Europe. There was the "Marie-Anne," the "Nouvelle" of 1880, which could do 27 miles per hour, the "Avant-Courrier" of the same year, and the "Rapide" of 1881.

All these vehicles were not only crude, cumbersome, and unattractive but, like a locomotive, required a fireman as well as a driver. For this reason Count Albert de Dion, with the mechanic Georges Bouton, worked out a little three-wheeler in 1883 which could be driven by one man. He followed it with others, faster and more economical. But the principal inconveniences remained: the driver had to stock water and coal, light the fire, wait for his car to get up steam and finally, he had to abandon all thoughts of travelling faster than the 24 miles per hour prescribed by law.

"There is a great need," Baudry de Saunier wrote, "to produce almost instantly and with little pressure the quantity of steam needed, and to do it with a strictly non-explosive boiler." Léon Serpollet, last of the great steam-car inventors, did precisely this, making the Paris to Enghien-les-Bains run in 1888 on a kind of tricycle which answered Baudry de Saunier's requirements. In 1890, with Ernest Archdeacon, he made the Paris-Lyon run in ten days. At Nice in 1902 Serpollet achieved a speed of 75 miles per hour.

Another motive force, electricity—which had begun to make its appearance on the railroads

120   *Léon Serpollet's first steam automobile, built in 1888.*
121   *Automobile built by Emile Levassor and René Panhard in 1891.*
122   *A Gottlieb Daimler automobile, 1895.*

Daimler and son in their first car, 1886 (123); 1889 Daimler car (124); von Loon's 1895 car (125); Karl Benz in his 1887 car (127).

123

124

125

126

127

Daimler taxi, Berlin 1898 (128); Stoewer's first car, 1899 (129); 1903 sports car "Italia" (126 and 130); a 1906 Peugeot (131).

128

129

130

131

The first Mercedes, 1901 (132); one of the first thousand Model T Fords, 1908 (133); design for a body, by Kellner, 1912 (134).

132

133

134

135

136

137

138

139

140

—also tempted those who believed in the future of the automobile. To be effective, the source of electricity had to be carried on the vehicle. Fortunately the newly-developed storage battery was just what was needed. An electric automobile by Nicolas Raffard appeared in Paris in 1883. About the same time an Englishman, Magnus Volk, brought out a similar car, while a carriage builder named Jeantaud produced one with a seven horsepower engine that could make 15 miles an hour. Later on, a racing car by Jeantaud achieved a world record—56 miles per hour. This was finally capped by Camille Jenatzy's electric "Jamais Contente," which did 65 miles per hour. Toward the end of the nineteenth century, when the gasoline automobile was still young, it seemed for a time as if the electric car might be the automobile of the future. Many were built—silent, powerful, and comfortable—and were a common sight up into the 1920's, especially in the cities. But electric traction had a serious defect: the batteries often weighed a ton, and the driver had to stop frequently to recharge them.

Eventually the noisy, vulgar, internal combustion engine won out. As with the wheel or the carriage, it is hard to tell who first invented it. As early as 1800 Philippe Lebon planned to explode a mixture of air and lighting gas in a cylinder to move a piston. Many others experimented with designs using various gases or volatile hydrocarbons as fuel; but the internal combustion engine first became commercially successful around the middle of the nineteenth century with the small gas engines of the French inventor Joseph Etienne Lenoir. The

next step was to compress the mixture before exploding it, an idea which was worked out in terms of the conventional engine by Beau de Rochas, in 1862. The idea was taken up in 1867 by Nikolaus Otto, who produced an engine twice as economical and twice as fast as Lenoir's. His four-cycle "Otto Silent" of 1876 led directly to the modern automobile engine. So far nobody had produced an internal combustion engine automobile, although both Lenoir and an Austrian, Siegfried Marcus, had made short-lived tests. Credit for the first gasoline-engine automobile seems to be divided between Gottlieb Daimler, one of Otto's assistants, and Karl Benz, both of whom ran their cars in 1886.

Daimler, hitting upon gasoline (then called "rock oil") as a fuel, produced a lightweight engine which he tested on a bicycle in 1885, thus unwittingly inventing the motorcycle. His first automobile was a four-wheeler with the front axle pivoted for steering. Benz's was a simpler three-wheeler, but had some features that remarkably anticipated the modern automobile, for instance, a rudimentary water-cooling radiator, electrical instead of flame ignition, and a differential gear. Its engine was a four-cycle, one cylinder affair with a belt transmission and a chain drive. Like the Daimler, its top speed was about ten miles per hour.

Daimler sold his patent to René Panhard and the engineer Emile Levassor, whose ambition it was to introduce the automobile to France. When the first tests were conducted in 1890 and 1891 the people in the cafés along the boulevards joked; but who cared? The first objective was to go from the Porte d'Ivry to

141 *Motorcycle built by NSU in 1902.*
As a means of transportation, the very
powerful motorcycle of today has
been largely replaced by the more modest
scooter and by small cars.

142 *During the early 1920s Americans began*
to buy automobiles in such quantities that
traffic jams, such as this one in Forest
Park, St. Louis, became a familiar sight.
143 *The British BSA motorcycle of 1920.*

143

the Viaduct of Auteuil and back without engine trouble, an objective that was soon achieved. After this the firm of Panhard-Levassor received its first orders, and was soon sharing them with Armand Peugeot who also used Daimler's patent.

The idea of holding a competition among all types of automobiles in existence—whether steam, electric, or gasoline—led to the first great race between Paris and Rouen—77 miles— organized in 1894 by Pierre Giffard of the *Petit Journal*. The winner was Count Albert de Dion, who averaged 13 miles per hour in his little steam car. In the following year (1895) a second race was organized, this time much longer and more difficult—Paris to Bordeaux and return, a distance of 744 miles. Steam was represented by one of Count de Dion's cars, two Serpollets, and Bollée's "Mancelle"; gasoline by a Panhard-Levassor and three Peugeots; and electricity by Jeantaud. Of the 21 vehicles participating, it was the Panhard-Levassor which won, completing the course in less than half the 100 hours anticipated by the organizers. The superiority of gasoline over steam and electricity was proved beyond a doubt. The race also proved the fact that an automobile, like a bicycle, not only could, but should ride upon air. For the tires of the Michelin brothers had been heavily committed in the race and had proved a success—even though they had to be changed by the drivers every 93 miles!

And thus began the infernal round, fascinating but murderous, right up to the Indianapolis race of today, the "24 hours" of Le Mans, of Monte Carlo, of other places—and it does not look as if it will ever stop. There was the Tour de France, the Paris-Berlin, the Paris-Vienna, the Gordon Bennett Cup, and the bloody Paris-Madrid race of 1903, in which Marcel Renault was killed. During competitions the roads from city to city, closed off, were turned into mad circuses filled with surging crowds. Yet progress resulted from all of this. Out of the noise and fury was born Germany's Taunus meet, Italy's Monza, England's Brooklands, and in the United States, the Atlantic City. From year to year the automobiles, under the stress of severe competition, were rapidly improved. Then there were rallies and competitions which sent automobiles around the world—the Paris-Peking of de Dion-Bouton, the "Croisière Jaune" of Citroën, the "Alger-le-Cap" and all the rest.

In Great Britain the Locomotive Acts of 1861 and 1865 had killed automobile transportation. But there was increasing opposition to the restrictions, led by such men as Sir David Salomons. During the race from Holborn Viaduct to Brighton the four miles an hour speed limit was repeatedly violated and everybody forgot about the man who was supposed to carry the red flag. The result was that the winner had to pay a variety of fines, and in 1896 the English Daimler company provided a man with a red flag to walk in front of every new car that left their works!

Then at last, in that same year, the House of Commons repealed the Locomotive Acts, and the automobile in England came into its own. There were great races like the "Hundred Miles of 1900." Soon the number of automobiles in Britain exceeded those in France.

144

The United States, lagging behind Europe, saw its first successful gasoline automobile— that of Charles and Frank Duryea—in 1893. It was a four-horsepower phaeton with a little engine just above the rear wheel. The American automobile industry dates from 1896, when the Duryea Motor Wagon Company produced 14 cars. The first Packard came out in 1899, the first Studebaker, made by the famous wagon-building firm, in 1904, the first Nash in 1918. But the real contribution of the United States was in mass production, and here the great Henry Ford was the star player.

Ford began with steam, but abandoned the idea. "To be seated on a high-pressure boiler which might explode and blow you sky high is not a pleasant thought." Everyone agreed. He put together his first successful "gasoline buggy" in 1896, then a series of cars followed— the "999", the "Arrow" and others—until he stopped to ask himself a question: "Which is better: to build a few expensive automobiles for the wealthy or a great number on a mass basis for everyone?" The answer, which was later received in Europe like a revelation, first by Citroën and then by others, is now history. The immediate result was the Model T Ford. In 1909 Henry Ford had written that "the automobile of the future must be superior to the present car to beget confidence in the man of limited means, and sufficiently lower in price to insure sales for an enormously increased output. The car of the future must be a car for the people... the market for a low-priced car is unlimited." How right he was! Between 1908 and 1928 more than 15 million Model T Fords were sold. In one day alone, during 1925, more than

9,000 were built. Who could do better? Or rather, who could do as well, for certainly this grand gesture by Henry Ford has inspired the competitors and successors who followed his example.

In Italy the first designs for a carriage that would run without horses—that old idea again—date all the way back to Leonardo da Vinci. But we had better start with Father Barsanti and Professor Mattenci, who together took out a patent for a gas engine in 1854. That same year Colonel Bordino built a car which can still be seen in Turin, while in 1894 Count Bernardi produced a small automobile. But the real beginning was in 1895, the year the celebrated Agnelli created the no less celebrated "Fiat" in Turin. As early as 1907 a Fiat, driven by Nazzaro, won a magnificent triple victory: the Targa Florio, the Sarthe circuit, and the Emperor's Cup. The road had been prepared for the elegant, thoroughbred automobile—so typical of Italy's automotive history—which includes such names as Lancia, Ferrari, Maserati, and Alfa-Romeo.

And so now at last the automobile had everything it needed: a four-cylinder engine, wheels of the same size all around, pneumatic tires (as well as the perennial puncture), a steering wheel, electric lighting, and even an electric selfstarter—thanks to the American, Charles Kettering, who introduced it in 1911. It was rather quiet now—far from the noisy "mad dog" that the newspaperman, Hugues-le-Roux, once threatened to shoot to pieces with his revolver. All that was left was to throw away the long coat, the goggles and gloves, the hat with its heavy veil and (while there was still room) drive off—drive off in complete freedom.

144   This powerful 350 cc
version of the popular
Blue Star series BSA
motorcycle appeared in 1935.
Since the invention of
the first real motorcycle
by Daimler in 1885, these
dashing machines have been
accepted by the young and
adventuresome as a symbol
of freedom and virility.
Leather-jacketed and helmeted
motorcyclists around the world
form a clique apart.
145   Heiner Fleichmann
whizzes around a dangerous
curve in the 1931 speed
tour around Scotland.

145

*146 Score of Arthur Honegger's "Pacific 231," based on
the composer's impressions of a high-speed, powerful
steam locomotive. First performed in Paris, May 18, 1924.*

The period from the late nineteenth century to the present has been a disturbing one, a period of mingled progress and dislocation, of unprecedented change matched by pressing problems. It has been a period of amazing technological progress, producing a vast array of inventions, all of them dedicated to the improvement of mankind; yet each invention has brought along with it new complications to plague us, and consequences entirely unforeseen. To take an ordinary example: everyone now has his automobile, but nobody can use it with the pleasure and freedom once anticipated. There are too many people, too many automobiles, and little choice is left between the snarl of the city's traffic and the menace of the open highway.

In this hurly-burly of convulsive change, in which the comic-book fantasies of today become the scientific realities of tomorrow, two old giants of land transportation—the railroad and the automobile—still hold their vital place. But the comic-books pay little attention to them, for like the wheel, far in the past, and then the horse-drawn carriage, they seem to be marking time. There is innovation and refinement, but no longer any real revolution.

It did not take long, it will be remembered, for steam to prove that it was capable of speed and power. Despite their big cow-catchers and bigger smokestacks, the American locomotives had reached speeds of 62 miles per hour by the mid-nineteenth century. In 1939 a record of 125 miles per hour was established on the London Midland Railway. As for size, no steam locomotives have ever surpassed the Union

147

147   *Aerial photograph reveals an involved network of tracks leading to the main railway station at Zurich. Heavy rail traffic, both freight and passenger, in and out of all the main terminals of the world requires complex systems of control and communication to avoid accidents and keep the trains running on schedule. Switching systems and automatic signals along the tracks, controlled by highly-organized centers of communications in the terminals, help to keep mishaps to a minimum.*
148   *Out of the night a train streaks past signal lights towards the station. From the first chuffing locomotives to the streamlined trains of today, railroading has always had an aura of romance and excitement.*

148

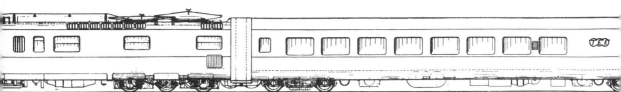

149 *Most modern and one of the fastest
of European trains, the Trans-Europe-
Express serves ninety of the major
cities of Europe, from Paris to
Munich, Marseilles to Hamburg.
Passengers travel and dine in comfort
while flashing across the countryside
at a maximum speed of 100 miles per hour.*

Pacific's giant "4000" class, while the Pennsylvania Railroad's first direct-drive steam turbine locomotive covered, with its tender, 123 feet of track.

But despite compound engines, superheated steam, and mechanical stoking with coal or oil, the steam locomotive was becoming a liability. Its efficiency was low, it was cumbersome, and its upkeep was time-consuming and difficult. After a certain amount of service it had to be sent to the shops for overhauling and cleaning. A more efficient, more flexible, and at the same time simpler power plant was needed.

Electric traction brought an elegant solution to these problems, at least for localities where electric power was cheap and abundant. A modern electric locomotive, 26 feet in length, weighs about 70 tons. A steam locomotive delivering the same power must weigh about twice as much. Moreover, the power on an electric locomotive is easily and simply controlled at all speeds, and the machine is very reliable and always ready to go. Finally, its acceleration is as smooth and rapid as that of an automobile.

A truly international effort, involving an Englishman, Barlow, two Germans, Jacobi and von Siemens, a Belgian, Gramme, an Austro-American, Tesla, as well as Swiss and French, went into the development of the electric locomotive. A halfway step was Heilman's 1895 steam locomotive in which the engine turned a dynamo that sent current to electric motors. About the same time the P.L.M. Company tested a battery-fed electric locomotive that could run at 46 miles per hour. But the batteries weighed an inefficient 20 tons. Clearly, there

was a problem that had to be solved if the electric locomotive was to be a success: it could not generate its own power, it could not be a mobile power station, but the power had to come from some outside source.

In 1893, on the slopes of the Jungfrau, the Swiss put into operation a railway that climbed in less than an hour from a height of under 7,000 feet to almost 10,000 feet above sea level. The current was supplied by an overhead line. Another mountain line, built in 1899, got its power from a "third" or electrified rail. The first idea proved to be generally more efficient, especially for higher voltages.

In the overhead line system the locomotive took its current from a double bronze wire suspended from a steel cable. Drawing current from the wire into the locomotive was the pantograph, a kite-shaped device mounted on the top of the locomotive and pressing upward against the overhead line.

The results from this system were astonishing. In 1954, running between Dijon and Beaune, the CC-7121 hauled 111 tons at 162 miles per hour. In 1955 two French locomotives—the BB-9004 and the CC-7107—ran between Lamothe and Morceux at 205 miles per hour, beating all world records. These were the fastest; the most powerful is a Swiss locomotive. It weighs 236 tons and develops more than 11,000 horsepower. While its level speed is modest, its traction is remarkable: it will pull 600 tons at 40 miles per hour up the Saint-Gothard. In the United States, locomotives of the 2CC2 type develop almost 5,000 horsepower and haul heavy expresses between New York and Washington at 90 miles

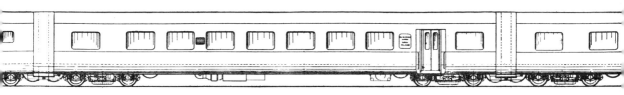

per hour. Elsewhere several electric locomotives have been teamed, giving more than 12,000 horsepower. But power in itself is no longer of great importance. Instead, the engineers are looking for the maximum power in the lightest and most economical package.

Along those lines that are not electrified, an important newcomer has appeared. This is the diesel-electric locomotive—in other words a diesel internal combustion oil engine coupled to a direct current generator, which supplies power to the electric traction motors. In a variant type the diesel is replaced by a turbine engine. The first diesel-electrics were used in the United States with high-speed streamliners as early as 1934. Two years later diesel-electric locomotives were hauling ordinary passenger trains, and in 1938 were introduced for freight service. The diesel-electric system is more flexible than that of the steam locomotive, while its fuel and operating efficiency is four of five times as great. Another advantage is the number of multiple-unit driving axles that can be concentrated under the control of one operator, allowing for quick train acceleration. These characteristics make electric drive far superior to steam for undulating profiles and frequent stops.

Moreover, servicing requirements for the diesel-electric at terminals are cut to the minimum because it has no boiler, and intermediate stops for engine supplies or machinery lubrication are not necessary. The high tractive effort available for acceleration permits close coupling of cars, and the dynamic brake assists in positive train control on long grades. Actually, the first cost of the diesel-electric is far higher than that of a comparable steam locomotive; but its many advantages more than compensate for the difference.

Electrification is extensive in Europe, where fuel is scarce and waterpower often abundant; but in the United States the opposite conditions prevail, and although there are huge electrified lines like that of the Pennsylvania Railroad, the diesel-electric is generally preferred, and today has just about driven out steam.

One result of the introduction of the electric and diesel-electric locomotives is increased speed. In order to reconcile the passengers to the stepped-up pace the railroads, well before World War II, began to provide a degree of comfort that would have left Monsieur Arago, the man who prophesied pleurisy and other horrors for earlier passengers, quite aghast. Thanks to hydraulic shock absorbers the suspension of the cars was much improved. Then there was air conditioning, with complete thermal and acoustical isolation. The comfort of France's "Mistral" express is so alluring that the majority of its passengers invariably go to sleep. American trains have buffet bars, smokers, cinemas, radios, and observation platforms—and the latest European trains are not far behind. In some trains the seats adjust in ten positions, the foot-rests in four! In the pendular car the centrifugal force of rounding a curve is neutralized by a double shell so that the passengers' feet remain firmly on the floor no matter how far the outer shell may lean.

The second problem posed by speed was that of the effect of the sudden application of the brakes. It was because the brakes had not been sufficiently applied that in 1895 the

150

150   The "Rio Grande," a streamlined
passenger train, winds its way through
a canyon in the American West.
Modern American trains provide new
comforts along with increased speeds
and attract many passengers who wish
to see the more scenic parts of
the country. Many trains, particularly
those that cross the continent,
provide glass-enclosed, rooftop
observation cars from which passengers
may admire the passing landscape.
151   Europe's version of the
de luxe passenger train, the Trans-
Europe-Express, crosses a bridge in
a snowstorm. This international system
of fast express trains has become
immensely popular among tourists and
businessmen in recent years.

151

Granville train tore like a rocket through the walls of the Montparnasse station in Paris, and after falling two storeys landed in the square. By a miracle there was only one victim. Today compressed air brakes, operating with disc brakes or shoes against the rims of the wheels, act quickly and with efficiency, at least up to a certain speed. To assure effective breaking at higher speeds, the electromagnetic system is available. Braking propellers have also been experimented with, and retrojets are under consideration.

The speed of modern trains, their weight, and the congestion of trains on the main lines have led to extraordinarily complex problems of safety, traffic, and switching control. Since it is becoming increasingly dangerous to rely upon human judgement, more and more automatic safety devices are being adopted. On board main-line locomotives, for instance, the visual danger signals are reinforced by audible signals. Another acoustical device consists of detonators which are automatically placed on the rails when a stop signal has been passed so that their firing will alert the train crew. An American system reproduces actions of the locomotive crew by means of a recording device, indicating speed, time, and brake valve manipulation. A "train control" system automatically stops the train without the engineer's intervention when caution signals have been disregarded, or danger signals overshot. Finally, the "dead man" system is used on electric locomotives with only one engineer. If he removes his hand from the operating position, or happens to fall where he is, brakes automatically stop the train.

The train alone profited from electricity, but in the aerodynamics race both the train and the automobile (not to mention the airplane) have been in close competition. The principle is well known: reduce air resistance by eliminating as far as possible everything that catches the air. The first streamlined trains were launched in Europe and the United States in the mid-thirties. Everything that stuck out was eliminated or enclosed, so that the train, like an arrow, could slip through the invisible wall of air ahead of it. Not only was there a gain in speed, but in economy too, for less power had to be expended than before. Adopting the same principle, automobile designers found that air resistance was far more important in holding back the vehicle than either mechanical or surface resistance. So first the useless accessories were discarded or rounded out, then the body itself was streamlined.

The automobile—how, our contemporaries ask, can one live without an automobile? Today there are some 100 million automobiles rolling on roads around the world: 60 to 70 million in America, some 20 million in Western Europe, two million in Africa, two million in Asia, somewhat over two million in Oceania and somewhat less than two million in the Soviet bloc. The most striking fact about the automobile today lies in its numbers. World production varies between eleven and twelve million a year. It has been estimated that France has one automobile for every seven inhabitants. Soon every family will have its own car. One? Not on your life! Salesmen today usually suggest two—one for Mr. Jones

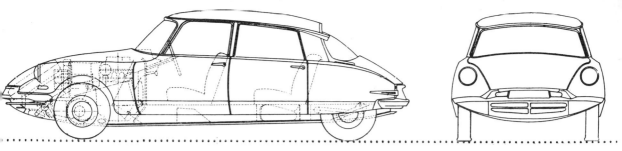

and another, smaller one, for Mrs. Jones. And why not a miniature one for the baby?

Let's not ask where and how all these vehicles are going to be used, but rather how we got into this situation. It was mass production, of course, the principle introduced by Ford. The assembly line and automation have resulted in a product of high quality and extraordinary complexity—more than 20,000 parts go into each automobile—which yet can be sold at a reasonable price.

Automobilists today want to go fast. Not of course as fast as the professional racers; but they would if possible like to go faster than the next fellow. But what actually is the speed situation today? The racers, in the avant-garde of the automobile industry—men like Fangio, Hill, Brabham, Trintignant, Gurney, Rodriguez, Moss and the rest—are going faster and faster: 125, 150, 190 miles per hour. From Le Mans to Monte Carlo, from Monza to Indianapolis we can hear the roar. The 500-mile Indianapolis race, above all others, is perhaps the toughest of all.

There are also pure speed records which have nothing to do with competition. In 1904 Rigoly reached a speed of 94 miles an hour, in 1909 Hemery made 125, in 1926 Segrave 168. The next year Segrave got up to 200 miles an hour and in 1929, 230. Next Campbell, Eyston, and Cobb appeared. Cobb made a record of 250 miles an hour in 1932, then 299 in 1935. Eyston then got over the 300 mark with 311 miles an hour in 1937. Cobb's last two records were enough to make him famous: 310 in 1938, and 391 in 1947. That is the situation at present. Speed is not the only difficulty; the vehicle must also be kept on the ground. If a racing car, hurtling over the Salt Lake flats, runs over a snail, or even an insect, it may well be sent flying into space.

But such speeds are not for the average automobilist. His eyes are rather upon the "family car" of tomorrow. It is difficult to guess what the automobile will look like a few years hence, or even if it will exist in its present form, for rapid changes are in the offing. Let us see what is being studied in the research laboratories. Pass over the excellent injection motor which enabled Moss with his Mercedes-Benz to run away with the "Mille Milles" of Italy in 1955. The immediate future seems to be in the hands of the gas turbine, which is very similar to the airplane's jet engine. The turbine is light, small in size, without vibration, and does not need a cooling system nor an ignition, except for a single spark plug for starting, and it can use almost any kind of fuel. The Americans with their General Motors "Firebird" and Ford "Volante," the French with their Renault "Etoile Filante," which reached a speed of more than 186 miles per hour at Salt Lake City, show what can be expected of a turbine motor. But general adoption of the turbine would mean a painful period of conversion that would considerably dampen the enthusiasm of the industry—a revision of all manufacturing methods, re-education of the workers, and of the drivers too. It is easy to understand why the industry prefers to sell its good old gasoline buggies.

Some designers have not yet given up electricity, and are searching for a battery that is light and powerful, and can rapidly be recharged. Such a battery may be a chemical

153 *Crack British racing driver, Sterling Moss, makes a controlled skid at 112 miles per hour during the 1959 Gran Primo d'Italia, which he won. At the wheel of his Cooper Walker, with its Coventry Climax engine, Moss was able to make such feats look easy. Actually they require long years of practice, steady nerves, and exceptional coordination.*

154 *The relatively new and inexpensive sport of karting, which began with American GIs in the Pacific, has attracted many adherents throughout Europe and the United States. Several classes of karts are being produced, the most powerful of which attain speeds of 100 miles per hour or more. The driver in this photograph is executing a difficult "two-wheel stand."*

154

155 At five o'clock in the morning, mountaineers Lionel Terray and Michel Vaucher set out to challenge the "Grand Capucin" in the French Alps — the peak which rises directly behind them. Even in this era of de luxe rail and automobile travel, there are regions which can be attained only on foot and by the most daring. And many people still prefer the old-fashioned ways, climbing on foot or on skis —"getting away from it all"— to pit themselves against the mountains and the elements.

156 But a variety of chair-lifts, cabin-lifts, and even helicopters and small airplanes are available to carry skiers, hikers, and picnickers to areas which were once the domain of mountain goats and a few agile humans.

156

*157   A parking lot in Brussels. The
problems of traffic congestion in all
the major cities of the world, not to
mention the troubles of the driver in
quest of a parking space, have led
many cities to introduce new programs
of building bypasses, expressways,
and big public parking areas.
158   Route 66, as it stretches toward
the Arizona horizon, presents an entirely
different picture of modern road travel.
The United States is covered with a
network of such roads, and a program
of building similar "autobahns," "auto-
routes," and "autostradas" throughout
Europe is well under way. Such roads
facilitate not only private automobile
travel, but also trucking, which has
taken over much freight transport from
the railroads.*

158

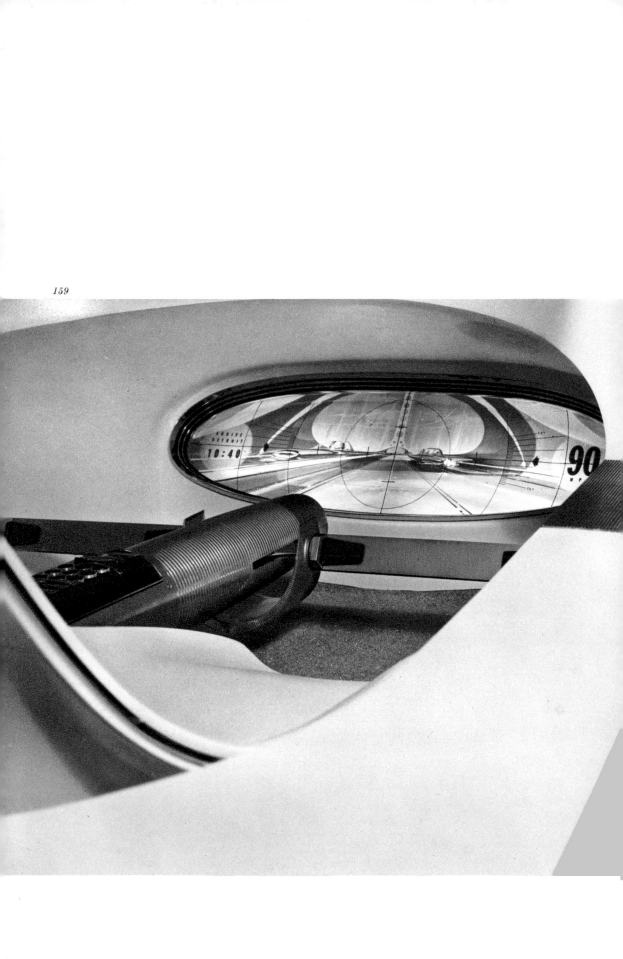

159 In the Gyron, full-sized "dream car" of the future developed by the Ford Motor Company, the passengers are able to relax while the fully automated vehicle whisks them safely to their destination.
A "snooperscope" or viewing screen enables passengers to watch the road ahead. Eventually it may utilize infra-red rays to give a clear picture even in bad weather. The screen may also show the speed of the vehicle and estimated time of arrival at a predetermined destination.
160 The Fulgar, developed by Simca in 1958, gives another idea of what the cars of the future may look like.

160

type that will not only provide a reserve, but a real current too. Then there are others who want to do away completely with the wheels, the steering, even the road. The Ford "Leva-car," for example, rises like a flying carpet and travels along on a kind of small air mattress beneath the vehicle, formed by jets of compressed air. Or there is the General Motors device in which one small lever replaces the accelerator, brakes, and steering. A flick of the finger forward makes it go faster, backward slows it down, left or right makes it turn. The last word is the remote-controlled, completely automatic car which, if it still has passengers, no longer has a driver. Finally, there is nuclear energy, still too complex, too heavy, too expensive. But the designers of trains and automobiles are beginning to dream of it.

In closing, one simple question. What has land transportation done to this small earth of ours, to the land itself, to the countryside? What after all makes the real charm of transportation? Today the earth groans under a jostling stream of 100 million cars. Tomorrow it will be 200 million, perhaps later 500 million. We may have to start dreaming of some other, cleaner landscape, on Venus perhaps, or Mars. "Across the ancient sea floor a dozen tall, blue-sailed Martian sand ships floated, like blue ghosts, like blue smoke" wrote Ray Bradbury in his *Martian Chronicles*. Mars was a dying planet; so, one day, may be this earth of ours: "The wind hurled the sand ship over the dead sea bottom, over long-buried crystals, past upended pillars, past deserted docks of marble and brass, past dead white chess cities, past purple foothills, into distance."

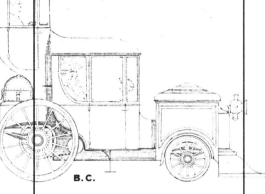

chronology

B.C.

5000 Parts of sledges dating from this period have been found in peat bogs in Scandinavia.

4000 The earliest representation of the wheel is shown on a Sumerian bas relief from around this time.

3500 The first pack animal, the ass, is used in Egypt and Sumeria.

2000 In Mesopotamia, the spoked wheel begins to replace the full wheel At about the same time the peoples of the Middle East adopt a Central Asian idea and begin to harness and mount the horse.

1700 A network of roads surrounds Babylon, leading toward the cities of Ecbatana, Susa, and Sardis.

1600 The horsedrawn chariot, introduced by the Hyksos, appears in Egypt about this time.

1500 Pharaoh Mentuhotep III opens a road to the Red Sea.

1200 Traces of Mycenaean roads from this period have been found in Greece.

450 Carthage builds a system of roads.

312 Appius Claudius lays out the Appian Way which eventually extends 132 miles.

220 Claudius Flaminius undertakes the construction of the Flaminian Way.

200 Chinese horsemen of the Han Dynasty begin using a rigid saddle.

120 The Romans extend their network of roads as far as the most distant provinces.

45 Heavy vehicles, too numerous in Rome, are forbidden within the urban enclosure by the "Lex Julia Municipalis."

27 Private enterprises for hackney carriages are created during the Augustan Age (27 B.C. - 14 A.D.).

A.D.

200 Toward the end of the later Han Dynasty, the Chinese equip their horses with breast harnesses.

476 Disappearance of the Western Roman Empire, under the impact of mounted barbarian invasions.

790 About this time Charlemagne, in his "Capitularies," requires those lords with toll roads not only to devote the tolls to the upkeep of the roads, but also to guard them. Thus he briefly arrested the deterioration of the old Roman road system.

799 Charlemagne opens three official postal routes, leading toward Germany, Italy, and Spain.

1176 The famous stone bridge of medieval London, superseding earlier wooden ones, is begun.

1177-
1188 The association of the
Pontifical Brothers builds the
Pont St. Bénézet at Avignon
over the Rhone. The bridge
is 3,152 feet long, has 22
arches. It is memorialized
in the well-known song,
"Sur le pont d'Avignon."

1200 The University of Paris, to
take care of the transmission
of money, letters, and
personal effects of its
students and faculty, sets up one
of the earliest of messenger
services, licensed by the king.

1284 Alphonse II, King of Spain,
creates a messenger service.

1294 Philip the Fair issues an
order forbidding women of
the bourgeoisie to ride in
carriages.

1345 Construction of the Ponte
Vecchio at Florence.

1400 The Incas of Peru build a
road system through the
Andes. One road is
1,860 miles long.

1455 At this epoch the average
speed for an official courier
is barely 37 miles a day.

1457 A Hungarian is supposed to
have invented the "chariot
branlant," the late medieval
"jolting carriage."

1502 The Thurn and Taxis family
is given the monopoly of the
postal services in Germany.

1553 Bookseller Charles Estienne
publishes the "Guide to the
Roads of France."

1592 Antonio da Ponte builds his
single-arch Rialto bridge,
which spans the Grand Canal
of Venice. It is 84 feet long.

1599 Henri IV names Sully
"Grand Voyer" of France
for the purpose of
reorganizing the country's
system of roads.

1599 The Marshal of Bassompierre
brings the first "caroccio," or
carriage, with glass windows,
to France from Italy.

1600 Simon Stevin builds a
carriage with sails for
Maurice of Nassau.

1616 Road guides for all of Europe,
similar to the one put out
by Estienne, are published in
Germany.

1625 The first carriages for public
use are put into service in
London.

1629 The Italian, Giovanni
Branca, publishes plans for
a vehicle powered by a
windmill. He also describes
a kind of steam turbine.

1645 In Paris, Nicolas Sauvage
rents out his "fiacres,"
complete with horse and driver.

1649 The Bristol Postal Service
begins to use a new and more
rapid vehicle on the line
between London and Dover:
the post-chaise.

1655 German watchmaker Stephen
Farffler builds a
mechanical vehicle propelled
by cranks.

1656 Cromwell in England names
a Postmaster and codifies the
schedules, lines, and rates
of the postal services.

1658 There are more than
310 "carrosses" in Paris at
this time. A few years later,
Parisians have access to five
public coach lines.

1667 First appearance of the
cabriolet. A light, two-wheeled
vehicle with leather hood,
English in origin, it became
all the rage in the
18th century.

1680 Dutch physicist Christiaan
Huygens makes a piston move
in a cylinder, exploding a
bit of gunpowder to provide
the force.

1690 Denis Papin describes a
primitive sort of piston
engine, which uses steam
rather than gunpowder.

1698 Thomas Savery of England
invents, patents, and builds
the first practical steam engine.

1712 Thomas Newcomen and John
Calley, two artisans from
Cornwall, build a reliable
steam engine for pumping out
mines.

1725 It is possible to travel the
434 miles between Paris and
Nîmes in six days, by
postchaise.

1757 The Schaffhausen bridge
across the Rhine, in northern
Switzerland, is constructed by
engineer Hans Grubermann.

1769 James Watt patents an engine which condenses the steam outside the cylinder.

1769 Cugnot's "fardier" is the first steam road vehicle.

1775 In France, Turgot creates the "turgotine," a fast stagecoach line for public transportation.

1775 Englishman Outram proposes the first horse-drawn tramway.

1775 Building of the first cast-iron bridge, to span the Severn, near Birmingham.

1784 William Murdock equips a model steam vehicle with an engine by Watt.

1790 The Count of Sivrac is said to have invented the célérifère, ancestor of the bicycle, in this year.

1801 Richard Trevithick and Andrew Vivian build a steam coach. In 1803 they test a steam tricycle in London.

1804 Oliver Evans tries out his steam vehicle, the amphibious dredge, "Orukter Amphibolos," in Philadelphia.

1808 The "Catch Me Who Can," a Trevithick locomotive, is exhibited on a circular track near Euston Square, London.

1813 William Hedley, builder of the "Puffing Billy," demonstrates that locomotive wheels adhere naturally to the rails, preventing slipping.

1815 John Loudon McAdam, while repairing the roads in

the county of Bristol, invents a new method of road surfacing, which proves successful and is soon adopted throughout Europe.

1818 The Baron Drais von Sauerbronn of Baden-Baden adds handle bars and springs under the seat to the Directory vélocifère, creating the "Draisine."

1825 George Stephenson begins construction of a railway connecting the coal mines of Darlington with the port of Stockton, in England. When the railway opened, in September 1825, Stephenson's "Locomotion No. 1" pulled 90 tons at 12 miles per hour.

1828 A railroad between St. Etienne, Roanne, and Lyons is built by the French engineer, Marc Seguin.

1828 Pecqueur invents modern automobile steering and the differential for steam carriages.

1829 Stephenson's locomotive the "Rocket" wins the Rainhill trails organized by the directors of the Liverpool-Manchester line.

1830 Peter Cooper's little American locomotive "Tom Thumb" wins a race against a horsecar, along the Baltimore and Ohio Railroad tracks.

1832 Englishman Goldsworthy Gurney runs his two-ton

steam coach on a four-trips-a-day schedule between Gloucester and Cheltenham.

1837 Laying of the first section of railroad tracks in the London area, on the Greenwich line.

1840 London is linked by rail to Southampton, Portsmouth, Brighton, and Dover. England now has 76 railway companies. In this year, the United States has 2,784 miles of railroad track, England 2,235, Germany 359, France 310, and Russia none.

1845 Robert W. Thomson invents the pneumatic tire, but no interest is shown in it.

1846 A locomotive of the Great Western Line hauls 100 tons at 62 miles per hour.

1855 A horse-drawn tramway line is opened in Paris, from the Place de la Concorde to Passy.

1859 Commercial exploitation of the first oil well, that of Edwin L. Drake at Titusville, in Pennsylvania, is begun.

1860 Frenchman Joseph Etienne Lenoir invents a small but practical internal combustion engine.

1861 Parisian Pierre Michaux constructs the first "vélocipède" by adding pedals to the Draisine.

1861 In this year, and in 1865, the Locomotive Acts are

passed in England, limiting the speed of steam-driven vehicles to four miles per hour, and requiring them to be preceded by a man carrying a red flag. For a time these acts slowed down the development of the automobile in England.

1863   Opening of London's "Underground," the first subway.

1865   In the United States, George Pullman builds his "Pioneer" sleeping car for fast night trains.

1867   New York City builds the first elevated railway, with tracks extending five blocks. A few years later, there are over five miles of elevated track in New York.

1868   Paris has 6,000 hackney carriages.

1868   George Westinghouse invents the compressed-air brake for use on railroads, thus adding an important element of safety to rail travel.

1869   The completion of the transcontinental railroad in the United States as the tracks from East and West are joined at Promontory Point, Utah, May 10.

1869   Champion cyclist James Moore, on his "Spider," does eight miles per hour in the Paris-Rouen race.

1871   Zénobe Gramme develops his pioneer electric dynamo.

1872   The first high wheel bicycle, the "Ariel," is built in England. In 1878 Frenchman Victor Renard builds a big-wheel bicycle seven and a half feet high (the usual high-wheeler had a five-foot wheel).

1872   The first monorail railway is shown at the exposition at Lyons.

1873   At San Francisco, the first practical tests of cable cars are made. The city soon has 105 miles of cable car tramways.

1875   Amédée Bollée's steam automobile, "Obéissante" makes a trip from Le Mans to Paris, a length of 142 miles, in 18 hours.

1879   Werner von Siemens runs a small electric train in an enclosure at the Berlin Exposition. This is usually considered to be the first electrified railroad.

1880   Thomas A. Edison conducts electric locomotive trials, on a half-mile-long track at Menlo Park, New Jersey.

1881   Siemens constructs the first electric tramway, on the outskirts of Berlin.

1885   Gottlieb Daimler equips a motorcycle with a lightweight gasoline engine.

1886   The first Daimler car, a gas-driven Victoria, is built in this year. By 1889

Daimler had produced a nearly definitive version of the internal combustion engine.

1886   Carl Benz produces his first automobile, a gasoline engine three-wheeler.

1888   John B. Dunlop invents his pneumatic tire.

1888   Nikola Tesla perfects an alternating current polyphase system, making AC current generally available for electric trains as well as for industry.

1889   By this time Frank J. Sprague, pioneer of electric tramways in the United States, has electrified more than one-half of American street car systems.

1890   Formation of the Touring Club of France.

1891   The Panhard-Levassor factory produces highly advanced automobiles, complete with rear-wheel chain drive, friction clutch, gear shift, magneto lighting, and foot and hand brakes.

1893   Opening of the electric cog-railway at the Jungfrau, in Switzerland. It climbs from 6,560 feet to 9,840 feet in one hour.

1893   Henri Desgranges, holder of the world record for the bicycle hour race, makes 21 miles in an hour at the Buffalo velodrome.

1894 The Count de Dion wins the Paris-Rouen race in his steam-driven automobile. Of the 15 entries, only his and one other are steam-driven. Although de Dion's is the fastest of the competing automobiles, (13 miles per hour) the superiority of the gasoline automobile over steam is clearly demonstrated.

1895 One of the first practical electric locomotives is tested at Baltimore, U.S.A.

1895 Léon Levassor wins the Paris-Bordeaux race in his "Number 5," covering the 744 miles at an average of 14 miles per hour. Again the superiority of gasoline-powered automobiles is proved.

1896 The Locomotive Acts are repealed by the House of Commons, spurring on the British automotive industry.

1897 The German engineer, Rudolf Diesel builds a reliable model of his famous internal combustion oil engine.

1899 The electric automobile "Jamais Contente" runs at 65 miles per hour, beating all records.

1900 In this year, the United States has 241,800 miles of railroad track, Russia 40,290, Germany 31,650, France 26,040, and England 22,940.

1902 Léon Serpollet, in his steam-driven "Easter Egg," attains the speed of 75 miles per hour, at Nice.

1906 Mariott, driving a steam automobile, increases the speed record to 125 miles per hour.

1908 Henry Ford begins the mass-production of his famous low-cost "Model T." In 20 years he built 20 million automobiles.

1913 There are already 108,000 automobiles in France.

1923 The Buick Company in the United States delivers its millionth automobile.

1925 The Ford factory produces 9,109 Model T's in one day.

1928 The Belgian, Vanderstuyft sets a bicycle-behind-motor-cycle record of 75 miles per hour.

1935 Major Campbell, in his famous "Blue Bird" racing automobile, reaches 299 miles per hour at Salt Lake City.

1939 A Pacific locomotive of the London-Midland Railway attains 125 miles per hour.

1947 Tubeless tires are first tested in the United States.

1947 Racing driver John Cobb achieves a speed of 391 miles per hour, a record still unbroken.

1954 The electric locomotive CC-7121 hauls 111 tons at 162 miles per hour between Dijon and Beaune.

1955 Two French electric locomotives do 205 miles per hour between Lamothe and Morceaux.

1956 An experimental Chrysler with turbine engine covers more than 3,000 miles across the United States.

1956 Renault's experimental gas turbine automobile "Etoile Filante" reaches a speed of more than 186 miles per hour.

1957 An elevated monorail is put into service on the outskirts of Cologne.

1959 The number of automobiles in the world exceeds 100 million.

1962 Swiss and Italian workers pierce through the final rock barrier in the Grand Saint Bernard tunnel, April 5. This tunnel, when completed, will connect Italy and Switzerland by highway. The 11,600 meter-long Mont Blanc Tunnel which, passing under the famed ski resort of Chamonix, will connect France and Italy by a two-lane highway, was pierced on August 14 of this year.

1962 Sixty-six years after the manufacture of the first American car, the U.S. automobile industry produces its 200 millionth motor vehicle, in December.

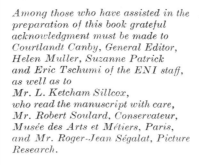

Among those who have assisted in the preparation of this book grateful acknowledgment must be made to Courtlandt Canby, General Editor, Helen Muller, Suzanne Patrick and Eric Tschumi of the ENI staff, as well as to Mr. L. Ketcham Sillcox, who read the manuscript with care, Mr. Robert Soulard, Conservateur, Musée des Arts et Métiers, Paris, and Mr. Roger-Jean Ségalat, Picture Research.

credits